61/7

CURATE'S EGG

Curate's Egg

Edited by

JOHN MARTIN

HIGHLAND BOOKS

ISBN: 0 946616 69 8

Cover illustration: Taffy Davies

Printed in Great Britain for
HIGHLAND BOOKS
Broadway House, The Broadway
Crowborough, East Sussex TN6 1HQ
by Richard Clay Ltd, Bungay, Suffolk
Typeset by Rowland Phototypesetting Ltd,
Bury St Edmunds, Suffolk

Contents

Foreword

by The Bishop of Bath and Wells
(The Rt Rev Dr George Carey)

Of course, the point about the proverbial Curate's Egg was that it was good in parts! Life is often like that; but so is the Christian ministry. In this book a number of curates share the stories of their curacies and reveal the good and bad experiences that have enriched their journey of faith. As a former theological college principal I can say that the essays represent a realistic and sobering account of how people feel when they leave college and settle down in the ministry to which they feel called. And yet it is a picture that may come as a surprise to many.

Students leave college as lay people and within a few days fasten that unfamiliar white band around their necks; a mark of separation. As lay people they may have held down very good jobs with good conditions and had a home of their own. Now they face the reality of low pay with, often, long hours and living in a home that goes with the job. I remember the strangeness of this new world when, nearly thirty years ago, I served my Title in Islington. I recall being in a railway carriage and watching with some amusement the large number of people who would not sit by my side – I apparently had a contagious disease, called 'vicaritis'!

But the essays not only help us understand the feelings that new curates have when they turn their collars round but they show the idealism and expectations changing as the reality of the ministry hits them. Some of the stories reveal the poor vicars that some curates had. This is an indictment of the church and the way we prepare people for a noble ministry. Bishops, and those who appoint, owe it to those who come with such huge desires to serve Christ with all their enthusiasm and love, to give them the very best of trainers. We need training staff who have not lost the love of ministry and who still burn with gospel-love and who still strain to serve their Lord with all their being. Academic flair and administrative ability – important though these qualities are – are no substitute for that primary quality of infectious commitment to the cause of Christ. Of course, it must be said, that in this fascinating book there are some splendid examples of wonderful training going on and some of the examples offer good models for erstwhile training vicars.

This leads me to reflect on the way we train people for ministry. Let me modify that. I don't think, to be frank, that we really do train people in the biblical way. You note the pattern of Jesus's training. He took twelve men under his wing; they watched him at work; they modelled their lives on his; gradually he left them to experiment and learn from their mistakes. There was a going and coming in ministry – a form of sandwich training – that led them into growth. These days in secular training this is called 'mentoring' but it was there in the ministry of Jesus and we should be seeking to emulate his pattern. Again, this comes across now and again in this volume but all too often curates are left too much to their own devices and so form bad habits that stifle the rich gifts they have been given.

I am personally disappointed that so many evangelical curates are let down by their incumbents. First, there is not always the discipline of daily prayer which forges a powerful spirituality. Second, evangelical curates are not often given the critical supervision in their study and sermon preparation that will lay down a firm foundation for the rest of their lives. How very ironic when such vicars and curates share the conviction that they are ministering God's word to others!

In short *Curate's Egg* is a stimulating exploration of the nature of the ordained ministry from the experience of people starting out. I commend it most warmly because it has a lot to teach the church, and the editor John Martin is to be congratulated for focusing our attention on a greatly neglected aspect of ministry.

Introduction

Not all that long ago the clergyman ascending his pulpit stood six feet above contradiction. He was the most educated person in his community and ranked high in its social pecking order. His vicarage was the centre for most of the welfare work in the area and he had oversight of local education.

Today there are many forces at work which seem to be challenging his (or her) sense of calling. Much of the social role of the clergy has disappeared with the development of the welfare state.

One of the sources of difficulty is the problem of folk religion. There are all sorts of pressures from people who want the church to bless their endeavours, endorse their politics, perform their rites of passage, and who insist that as far as the fabric or worship of the church is concerned, 'as it was in the beginning, is now and ever shall be.'

Then within the gathered community of the church, the growth of a new consciousness among the laity is proving to be double-edged. Lay people have taken to heart the call to exercise the gifts of the Holy Spirit and to assert the 'priesthood of all believers.' That is all to the good. Yet in the process many of these people are apt to deny the validity of any 'special calling' to be clergy in a church operating on the basis of New Testament principles.

This is the scene into which the new recruit – the curate or parish deacon – is being thrust. It is requiring clergy and laity together to rethink the nature of ministry and some-times renegotiate their respective roles.

In this volume, an assortment of curates and parish deacons – men and women from different parts of England – tell it like it is about full-time ministry in the early years. The book is published in the hope that it will help remove some of the mystery of what the clergy do from day to day. It is also published in the hope that it will encourage people who may be wavering about offering to serve God in this vocation to affirm that 'the church needs people like me.'

It is dedicated to the current generation of curates and deacons of the Church of England. These are momentous times. The established church has before it an enormous catalogue of challenges to be faced and overcome. Their contribution will have a significant bearing on whether or not it succeeds.

As the editor may I express my appreciation to all who have been associated with the creation of this book. To the team of contributors, to Steve Walton and Di Lammas from the Church Pastoral Aid Society for advice about some of the key issues and some helpful introductions, to the Rt Rev Michael Scott-Joynt (Bishop of Stafford and a former Diocesan Director of Ordinands) for a helpful guide to the church's selection and training processes, to Tim Anderson who helped with copy-editing, to Hannah Scott-Joynt who cheerfully assisted with research, and to Edward England for encouraging me to take up one of his many good ideas, a hearty thank you.

John Martin

Chapter One

OBEYING THE CALL

by

Bob Jackson

A man who is good enough to go to heaven is good enough
to be a clergyman

Samuel Johnson

We were watching the bishop baptise a baby in Norwich Cathedral. It was a fascinating experience as both my friend, David Hayes, and I were deacons at a Baptist church. 'Have you ever thought of going into the ministry?' asked David. I hadn't. 'It's a nice thought,' I replied. 'I get more fulfilment in my church work than advising in Westminster, but I could never afford it!' As an economist I was already earning more than the bishop, let alone a theological student or curate. Christine was expecting our first baby and I had responsibilities.

But the thought never left me. Months later, after Matthew our son had been born, I mentioned it to Christine. 'I've always wanted to be a vicar's wife,' she replied to my astonishment. It had been an ambition she had buried when she married a civil servant, but now it was out in the open. We began to take the idea seriously. After praying and taking advice from older Christians we formed a plan. Even though we were then Baptists, our desire, we realised, was to enter the Anglican ministry. Partly this was because we both had Anglican roots, and partly because we believed in the baptism of children of Christian parents. But it was also in part inexplicable. The plan was to test out whether this strange desire was a result of a genuine call from God or not.

So I chose the approach to the Church of England that would most invite rejection! Instead of going gradually, talking to local clergy and enlisting support I wrote direct to our bishop, a very 'churchy' Anglican who didn't normally deal with potential ordinands who were Baptists. He wrote back the expected reply saying it was totally impossible for someone with so little commitment to the C. of E. and who went to a Baptist church to proceed towards ordination. But right at the end, he suggested I go and see a rural dean! Eventually I was sent off to a Selection Conference and the call of God was confirmed by the call of the church.

One of the hardest things in accepting the call was to accept the loss of status and income it entailed. We had gradually come to realise that going into full-time ministry was at heart an act of self-sacrificial obedience. It would bring comparative penury, hardship and pain as well as the privilege of ministering Christ. Although we had no assured income when we left London for St John's College, Nottingham, the penury was not as bad as we had feared. Living 'in faith' quickly taught us we could trust God for our needs, even though the loss of income would be a permanent sacrifice. God had called us so he would provide.

For instance, there was the house. We had toured Nottingham all weekend looking for one we could afford. Eventually we visited a house that was available to rent. The owners were welcoming and gave us food and drink. But it seemed too nice and too expensive for us, so we sat outside in the car and prayed. 'Lord, is this the right house or should we move on to look at some more?' I felt compelled to open my Bible at random and read the first verse my eye alighted on to find God's answer. This isn't normally a recommended technique. But just this once it was the right thing to do. I opened at Luke 10.7:

> Remain in the same house, eating and drinking what they provide, for the labourer deserves his wages; do not go from house to house.

Through such experiences we learnt to trust God, that he knew what he was doing in calling us to the full-time ministry. He had directed us to the C. of E., to St John's, and to the house where we should live. Now he would direct us to the curacy he had prepared for us.

But we weren't so holy as to hang around waiting for a curacy to drop from heaven. Being northerners we wanted to return to the north and anyway, my London diocese told me there would be no job for me there. So while at college I transferred my 'sponsoring' diocese to Sheffield. This was partly in response to Christine saying, 'I've always wanted to live in Sheffield.' It was another inexplicable instinct in her that had been buried when marrying a London civil servant. For me, Sheffield was home and I had a strong feeling for both its spiritual and its economic state. We felt drawn to it, and still do.

A year before my college course ended, I met the new Bishop of Sheffield and he sent me to see the parish of Christ Church, Fulwood, and to meet its vicar, Philip Hacking.

The visit seemed to go well, although being driven round the parish by Philip was a memorable experience and I made a mental note not to accept lifts from him again! The visit to the wardens was slightly daunting, especially for Christine, with everyone on their best behaviour in the big Fulwood houses. It was impossible to see at that point the warm and lasting friendships that would develop. A few days later, Philip wrote to invite us to join him and we spent a day in prayer and fasting to decide our response.

There were several things against going to Fulwood. It was distinctly posh. We were not going to meet many ordinary people who didn't have degrees or money behind them. Philip in particular and the parish in general were quite well-known and we wondered whether we would get the experience we needed for ordinary parish work later. Fulwood was also in a straight evangelical mould we had grown a little away from. We would have felt more comfortable with a church more open to renewal and to the rest of the Church of England.

It was clear that Philip did not intend to 'train' me in the conventional way because he was fully stretched in his parish and wider ministry. We would not be meeting to say the daily office, a freedom which for me was certainly an attraction. But even if we were not going to live in each other's pockets, it would still be vital to get on well with my vicar, and I felt, rightly, that I would.

Philip's great gifts were in preaching and evangelism, and he had other responsibilities outside the parish, for example as chairman of a missionary society. All too often, people, including curates, have unrealistic expectations of vicars, expecting them to fulfil all their varied parish roles to perfection as well as the extra things that come their way. But no one is gifted in every direction, and no one has forty-eight hours in the day. Philip seemed to fit far more into his twenty-four hours than most vicars, but I would have to learn from him as a role model rather than a trainer, and I would not necessarily see all that much of him. It would be up to me to learn my own lessons along the way, and this suited my independent temperament.

We very much wanted to get experience of a large church from the inside, to understand how it worked and its dynamics. With an electoral roll of a thousand, Fulwood certainly fitted the bill. After our day of praying and fasting we felt it was God's place for us and accepted the offer.

But we did add a condition. The house was essentially a good one, but had been allowed to deteriorate internally. The kitchen was primitive, the central heating didn't penetrate upstairs or into the attic where the study would need to be, and the electric wiring was so bad that bare wires could be seen behind some of the power points. It seemed wrong that the state of the curate's house should be so out of line with the immaculate state of the rest of the parish plant, so we asked for it to be put right. The wardens agreed and the work was put in hand with professionalism and generosity. The kitchen was rebuilt, the wiring dealt with and some decorating done. But the attic study never did get central heating, and many was the winter morning I shivered in it writing sermons with my gloves on while the ice gradually melted from the inside of the windows!

We moved a few weeks before ordination. We were working steadily round the house decorating and had got half way through painting the toilet when Matthew and Ruth went down with viral meningitis and I went down with mumps. Christine was in the middle of marking geography O level papers, and Ruth spent a week at the nearby hospital in isolation. It wasn't the best preparation for ordination! I spent the days I should have been on the pre-ordination retreat with my cheeks like hamsters' pouches watching Wimbledon on the TV at home. The day before the service I went to the doctor to see if I was still infectious or could be allowed out into the cathedral. He spent about twenty minutes consulting large volumes and phoning specialists and eventually decided I probably wouldn't give the bishop mumps. So I could go and be ordained. When I left Fulwood, the toilet was still a mixture of brown and lurid blue!

My time was taken up with the usual variety of clergy activities, magnified in my case by the size and ethos of the church. My morning sermon would be preached to about seven hundred and the evening one to up to five hundred; the congregation would include professors and theologians and people with their Greek New Testaments open. They were all kind and supportive, but time and care had to go into those sermons. Then I often had to do the Wednesday evening Bible reading – forty-five minutes of detailed exposition. There were plenty of weddings, funerals and baptisms; the '20s group' we looked after which met for tea at our house every Wednesday; the homegroups, the weekly hospital visiting every Tuesday afternoon at Lodge Moor Hospital where we were chaplains; the weekly staff meeting, the home communions, the large number of church groups, and many other things to stop me being bored.

It was the ethos of the church as much as its size which contributed to the hectic life. Sometimes it seemed that evangelicalism was more about doing things for God than allowing him to do things with you. I felt pressure to fill up all my time with activity rather than to deepen my spirituality. I was partly to blame myself, being an activist by temperament. It was too easy to fill every waking hour with preparation, visiting, and meetings. It was new and fresh and exciting and I had well-charged batteries to keep me going. But full-time ministry is a marathon race not a sprint. After six years in my own parish I am still trying to be less of an activist and to follow my theology instead, which tells me to listen to God more, to replenish spent batteries with prayer and retreats, to take a proper day off, and to enjoy the delights of ordinary life as a whole human being without the clergy machine part of me feeling guilty.

Curates, by and large, do not enjoy a high social status either in the church or outside of it. When it comes to weddings and funerals people prefer the vicar, and it can be very frustrating to those who have had responsible jobs in the past to be treated like schoolboys by the church authorities and the parish. But the folk at Fulwood did help me to feel respected and responsible, with a proper job to do, and their generosity made us better off than most curates and many incumbents. For instance, there was the parishioner who saw me trying to push start the beat-up Cortina and bought us a new one!

Being a curate in a large church which had always employed curates meant that there was a full and well defined role for me. I had to fit the job description, to help keep a busy parish humming. There was little room for personal initiative. I had realised this before going to Fulwood, and in many ways I didn't mind. Rather I wanted to find my way around a large church and understand what made it tick.

I would have felt frustrated if I couldn't have made any sort of personal mark at all so I did try to find a few things of my own to do. These ranged from writing a small book about Christian perspectives on Government economic policy to building a model railway in the cellar and inviting the railway enthusiasts in the congregation to monthly railway evenings. I also spent time encouraging homegroups to develop and multiply, feeling that they met many people's needs better than the more impersonal and cerebral central midweek meeting. As a curate I couldn't change the structures of the church, even if I thought they were not ideal, but I could strengthen the ones I felt were valuable and in need of development.

The homegroups were based on areas, and we joined our local group, mainly based on residents in our road. The majority of neighbours were Christians, and the children playing out together also met each other on Sundays in church and at homegroup events. This made Silver Birch Avenue a happy place to live, with a sense of Christian fellowship and neighbourliness. I now have an ambition that in each road in my own parish so many of the residents will become Christians that they will dominate the whole feel and ethos of the place.

Another advantage of a curate in a large church is being a member of a staff team rather than the vicar's assistant. This meant I had several colleagues to learn from and have fellowship with. Indeed, I often saw more of Greg Thomson, our youth worker, or James Forrester, minister in charge of our daughter church, than I did of Philip. The weekly staff meetings consisted of Bible study, prayer for the parish, and business, with little opportunity for personal sharing. Building friendships with the other staff members and their wives was therefore doubly important to us.

From a large number of capable and committed Christians of all ages in the church we found friendship and fellowship, receiving from them as well as ministering to them. This richness of Christian life was the chief joy of being part of a church like Fulwood. Some of our happiest times were being part of the leadership team on the annual Youth Fellowship holidays and the 20s group houseparties. One summer in North Wales I had arranged a trip to a castle for the young people to watch a display of medieval jousting. Unfortunately, there was only one horse brave enough to take part! Rehearsing late at night the inevitable sketch of how to joust with only one horse was memorably hilarious, as were the teenagers getting out of bed to complain that the noise we were making was keeping them awake!

We enjoyed being members of a homegroup without having to do all the giving, and there was a seemingly endless supply of delightful Christians to get to know. It was, in the end, an embarrassment of riches because the sheer numbers made it hard to give much time to anybody. Too few of all the potentially fruitful relationships, therefore, had much depth and this we found frustrating.

Although my job was clearly marked out, Christine's wasn't. She had abilities and experience to offer, but in every sphere there were always several members of the congregation equally able. She wasn't needed in the sense she would have been in most churches. The call to ministry was felt jointly between us. It was easier for me to be fulfilled than it was for her. She hadn't given up her former life to be a comfortable spare part and curate's housekeeper in a church that could manage perfectly well without her.

After a while, however, Christine did find herself something useful to do. There seemed a gap in what the church had to offer new Christians. She began to lead a 'Basics Group', which went through the fundamentals of the faith and discussed the difficult issues raised. She wrote the course material and led the groups, which, with typical Fulwood people, tended to be quite stretching intellectually. The result for Christine was not just the satisfaction of giving new and questioning Christians a solid foundation and then seeing some of them grow into leadership positions, but also the pleasure of new friendships formed.

There were, of course, other Christians of leadership quality in the church who were not being stretched as perhaps they should. This was not for want of trying by Philip or ourselves but an almost inevitable consequence of our situation. Most of the middle class housing in Sheffield is concentrated into the South West corner. This is where the middle class church-goers congregate. Fulwood was a church well known to many graduates moving to Sheffield, partly through Philip's ministry at university Christian unions. The church had a large proportion of natural leaders

and was under-using them. Yet this was in a city with about
the lowest proportion of church-goers in the country. Apart
from a handful of churches in the South West (of which
Fulwood and St Thomas's, Crookes are the best known)
most churches in Sheffield were struggling.

That this was resented by other clergy was quickly appar-
ent as I started to meet them. Being curate of Fulwood took a
lot of living down! As a vicar now on the other side of
Sheffield I still feel the problem of the few large churches
hoarding the leaders the rest of us feel we need. But there was
another side to it as well. The size and resources of Fulwood
meant it could achieve things beyond smaller churches. The
preaching ministry helped settle and deepen the faith of
generations of students. The large, professionally run children's and youth groups meant that far fewer teenagers were
rejecting their parents' faith. The church was turning out
generations of Christian teenagers. My confirmation group
for 14-year-olds had up to forty members each year. The
church was providing teams of people to do parish missions
with Philip all over the country. Its annual missionary gift
days provided large sums for ambitious projects. In many
ways a large, well resourced church like Fulwood had
the power to achieve things that even a number of small
churches together could not.

We felt this personally two years after leaving Fulwood
when our son Matthew, aged ten, was killed in an accident
on holiday. Our friends at Fulwood shared our grief along
with our newer friends from St Mark's, and contributed to a
fund in memory of Matthew that went to a boys home in
Calcutta. Philip rang up one day to say that the Fulwood
PCC would pay for us to go to Calcutta and meet the boys.
The story is told in *Matthew* (Highland Books, 1987). This
sharing in our bereavement deepened our relationship with
friends from Fulwood even though we now lived apart from
them. We were sustained through the dark months by a great
barrage of prayer, much of it from Fulwood. That prayer
alone amply repaid anything we had given to them.

My new curate at St Mark's, Philip Dobson, was ordained

recently at Sheffield Cathedral. His wife, Jill, has written about themselves in our parish magazine under the heading 'You're getting more than just a curate'. How right she was! As well as Philip, Jill and their four boys (aged between four and eleven) have also joined our church fellowship and are finding their way about in it. The upheavals and adjustments asked of clergy children are as great as those of their parents as they move from the secular life to college to curacy to the next job all within a few years.

Matthew was five and a half when we went to Fulwood and Ruth was three. One factor weighing on our minds in agreeing to go there was the welfare of the children. My parents lived in nearby Ecclesall and so they would be near to grandparents for the first time. The area was a lovely one for children growing up. Ruth and Matthew had three happy years and enjoyed their life in the church. The worst aspect of having Dad as a curate was Sunday mornings. Often I would go out for the 8 a.m. Communion as they woke up, and then stay out for the main services at 9.30 and 11 a.m. The 11 o'clock service was a repeat of the 9.30 to get everyone in. It would be well after 1 p.m. before I could get home. Christine had to struggle like a single Mum to get the two out of the house and up the hill to church for the 9.30 service and then used to bribe them with a Mars Bar each after the service to compensate for the loss of Dad.

There were compensations for the children, not least being the chance to join in the fun at the 20s group and youth fellowship holidays, and also the 20s fork supper. Every Wednesday by long tradition the group (mainly 18s to 35s and single) congregated at the curate's house for supper. They cooked it themselves in our kitchen and packed into our lounge, as many as thirty at a time, to eat. There was the occasional mess on the cooker or carpet to clean, but we all enjoyed the experience! The group made a fuss of the children for whom it was a weekly highlight. They were also a source of excellent and popular baby sitters.

One of the group, Nicki, babysat for the first time in his life one Christmas while we took Matthew out carol singing with the church round the parish. When he discovered Ruth was already asleep and that babysitting involved cake, a warm fire and a good book he was an instant convert!

Throughout the curacy years, Matthew especially, being older, developed a Christian faith and became an avid supporter of TEAR Fund, prone to pouncing on the 20s group with his collecting box. The curacy experience for Ruth and Matthew was happy and positive.

A common, probably universal, problem for curates is what they do when they find themselves disagreeing with their vicar. Provided the differences are not fundamental these ought to be creative situations. I try to encourage my own curates to work out what they would do differently from me if they were vicar and to try out their own ways of ministry. It seems as good a way as any of helping them work out what sort of vicars they will be later on. For this to work well the curate needs to be in basic sympathy with the vicar's theology and to have a good and trusting relationship with him. Fundamental disagreements and personality clashes are destructive. The curate also has to learn to accept the vicar for who he is and not imagine he can change him overnight; and to accept he has neither the power nor the time to turn his parish upside down. The vicar needs to be personally secure and not feel threatened by another clergyman who sees his parish differently.

There were aspects of ministry where my approach would have been different from Philip's, but we had enough common ground and a good enough personal relationship for them not to cause too many problems. For me, working out what I would do differently and what I could do the same was part of my learning experience. I learned to love him for who he was and the gifts he had rather than criticise him for what he was not and for what he didn't have the time to do. My main problem was the familiar border country where evangelicalism meets renewal.

We went to Fulwood with an experience of the renewal movement and a basic sympathy with its worship ethos, acceptance of spiritual gifts, healing ministry, body ministry, and openness to many different strands of spirituality. Even though we had grown up in it, we no longer quite fitted with the more tightly defined and traditional evangelicalism that Fulwood represented. I determined not to make this a big issue, but as a different emphasis emerged in sermons and conversations, the more charismatic members of the congregation began to come to me with their frustrations and complaints. It was important to handle the situation without encouraging a charismatic opposition group while not denying my own beliefs. This I tried to do by counselling patience for the church and pointing out ways in which renewal was seeping in, and by channelling energies into areas where the church as a whole was open, for example, into a healing prayer group. I'm not sure this always worked, but it strengthened my resolve to love, accept and understand Christians at different places along the charismatic road and off it.

An overwhelming fact about a standard three year curacy is its brevity. No sooner had I begun to feel at home swimming about in the large lake than it was time to leave it to be a bigger fish in a smaller pond. Working out the sort of job and place to move to next, and then finding it, is part of life as a curate. This is because a curacy is always both a job in itself and a preparation for what is to follow. The first year had been finding my feet and getting started, the second year had been relatively settled, and what there was of the third year involved the business of moving away. Moves from first curacies to other jobs cannot be timed with precision, and I began looking in the autumn. By March, two and three quarter years after ordination, I was vicar of another parish.

I began by taking two or three Sunday mornings off from Fulwood to sample life in other local churches. We needed to think and pray about the sort of church we should go to. Should it be an ordinary, struggling parish church? Should it be somewhere with a name for being charismatic, or evangelical? I hadn't had much chance at Fulwood to get out and about in other churches and so felt the need to remind myself of what they were like. We ended up thinking that probably we were called to an ordinary parish rather than an established success or one with a strong label.

I got in touch with various patronage societies and went to look at a parish in the West Midlands, but we felt no sense of call to it. We didn't really want to leave Sheffield, but were prepared to look elsewhere. The visit confirmed to us our sense of call and vision for Sheffield.

The move to St Mark's started with a chance conversation with another clergyman in the Fulwood vestry just before a service. He had been to look at a parish the other side of Sheffield but decided it wasn't for him. I wasn't sure it sounded like it was for us either, but Christine encouraged me to investigate. The next day I was at a conference at the Diocesan Conference Centre at Whirlow, and happened to sit at lunch next to David James, Vicar of Ecclesfield and patron of the parish in question, St Mark's Grenoside. I had never met David before and the coincidence seemed too great to ignore. We met the wardens and the PCC and had our usual day of prayer and fasting before big decisions. During that day we were given a vision for the job God wanted us to do at St Mark's and a definite call to go there. As God had moved us from London to college to curacy he was now moving us to the place he had ready for us. We obeyed the call and accepted the living.

Christine's ambition had been to be a vicar's wife, not a curate's! The curacy had been a last step along the way, a step which was in itself fulfilling, an apprenticeship and experience for the real thing. A curacy moulds the curate and his wife for their future ministries. The job God had given us for the longer term was now to begin. But we would always be grateful to Philip and to Fulwood for the rich experience of being with them in the privileged role of curate and wife.

Bob Jackson is vicar of St Mark's, Grenoside, Sheffield.

Chapter Two

ADJUSTING TO A NEW LIFE

by

Graham Dodds

I have been determined to be ordained longer than I can
remember, and I had very likely got quite used to the idea
before really knowing what it meant

William Temple

It was August 1st 1984. I had been ordained a deacon in Southwark cathedral just one month previously and on the advice of Richard Thomson the Vicar of Reigate, (an ex-Cavalry officer in the regular army) I had taken a month's leave after the frantic packing of bags and saying goodbyes in Bristol. Theological College was now behind me and a potential forty years of ministry were ahead. As I woke that morning I sensed a feeling of excitement mixed with apprehension. For the first time, I realised I had not the slightest idea what a minister in the Church of England does for a living. Would I be involved in some great pastoral crisis by the end of the day? Would I be called to the bed of someone breathing their last, wanting comfort and assurance?

As I walked down the street in my crisp new clergy shirt, I felt the sharp cutting edge of the plastic collar, so neatly inserted, rubbing on my chin. A thorn in the neck to remind me of my calling. My first appointment was at the old people's home just 200 yards from where my wife and I were staying, but the agreement had been to meet at the vicarage. Richard greeted me and complimented me on my appearance. I grinned a rather embarrassed smile as it came home to me that I was the new boy. I was secretly glad that we were to go to give communion to the fifty or so elderly people in the home. This was real ministry and I was going to meet real people. Later, as the service concluded, I was elated. This was what I had looked forward to for more than nineteen years.

It was in a dark and mystical Catholic church in the North East of England, at the age of seven, that I'd first felt an attraction to the ministry. As the priests intoned the Latin service in a blaze of light at the altar I had knelt with my school chums in the musty pews and marvelled at the glory of God. It was there on a Friday afternoon whilst attending Benediction that I had decided that I wanted to be a priest like the ones I had seen. I wasn't a Catholic, but I was in a Catholic school run by nuns and although I had no idea how to become a priest, I knew that one day I would be one.

It all came back to me in the old people's home as I read the gospel and administered the wine. So, what next? A funeral, a pastoral visit, a baptism interview? Actually, for me – nothing! Richard bade me farewell and went off to prepare a sermon and reply to some letters and I found myself sitting in the garden wondering what to do. Pauline, my wife, was surprised to see me doing nothing when she returned from shopping. 'Finished for the day?' she asked sarcastically. The truth was that I had! The great irony and certainly the greatest initial problem had begun. Working without a timetable, having to organise my own time was the biggest problem I faced for at least twelve months. It's still a problem now but other anomalies have superseded it in importance. There I was, raring to go, sitting in a sun-drenched garden on a lounger, baking in the heat with the plastic collar now burrowing itself into my flesh. I tried to read a commentary but my mind was far too busy to study. Is this really what it's all about? Can it really be true that clergy only work on Sundays with a few bits and pieces thrown in during the week?

A few months later a friend from college commented in a letter that the three days off after Christmas meant more to him than the fourteen weeks' vacation in the summer at theological college. How true, I thought. Those initial few days of hanging around wondering what to do were very quickly lost in the mêlée of activity that deluged us in September.

One thing that I have always enjoyed is the weekend. That 'Friday night feeling' with its anticipation of freedom was always precious to me. I never fully appreciated what it was all about until it disappeared, but disappear it did, overnight. Thursday is an odd day to take off. Wednesday becomes Friday and Friday becomes Monday without church in between and without a Monday morning feeling. It all gets very confusing to the body and it took about a year to sort out. My first Christmas almost paralysed me. It certainly left me with a feeling that if I sang one more carol I would scream. By the ninth Carol Service I longed for Epiphany.

Easter needs stamina. Holy Week wrecked my day off and by the Sunrise Service at 6.00 a.m. on Easter morning I'd had it. Inexperienced as I was I'd booked a week of leave beginning Easter Monday – something I've learnt is not ideal. I returned to work the Monday following to find my colleagues rested after a 'quiet week' preparing for *their* break away from the parish and leaving me to hold the fort. It wasn't the best week I've spent. I was hardly away from the phone and I dealt with my first enquiry about a possible exorcism and ministered to a dying man at his bedside in intensive care.

Before ordination a friend from college had given me a card with a text on it, 2 Corinthians 13.4: 'For to be sure, he was crucified in weakness yet by God's power we will live with him to serve you.' It's become a sort of motto for me, which I remind myself of as I seek to serve God in the parish. It was particularly relevant that week.

As time has gone on I've learnt to realise that people are individuals and that they are more important than any bright ideas I might have for the church. Take for instance the youth leader who left his post in the church partly because of a disagreement with me as to his style of leadership. It wasn't until I attended his bedside in hospital when he was very seriously ill, we prayed and he was miraculously healed, that I began to understand that God loves people more than styles of leadership or structures. I wasn't naive. I just needed to learn it at a gut level. It's very easy to try to run a church like a business. Having just returned from America I recognise the tension between being a well-managed business in order to enable the church to function well, and being a loving, caring family. As Verna Dozier and Celia Hahn, two American lay theologians put it, 'A funny thing happened on the way to the Kingdom, the church, the people of God, became the church, the institution.' How sad but how true. Growth is always untidy, and who but the most whole person can resist tidying it all up into neat categories of people, boxed up and bound up by the status quo. If this curate had been allowed to have his way too much in the earliest days then Reigate Parish Church would have ended up as one enormous filing cabinet!

There are some strange anomalies for ministers in the Church of England. One Friday afternoon found me at the crematorium taking the service of an elderly gentleman who, as far as I know, had never set foot inside the church. On Saturday I was in church marrying a couple who had attended church two or three times to hear their banns read but again had rarely seen the inside of the building. During the Sunday morning service I baptised a baby, needless to say she hadn't formed a long standing relationship with us, but similarly neither had her parents. Yet in all three cases I was privileged to share in these intimate moments of the life experience. I found myself punch drunk by the end of the weekend trying to sort out whether I was empathetically sad, happy or just plain mixed up. These occasions are of course bread and butter to all ministers. Some parishes have quite an imbalance. I've heard stories from friends in the inner city of 150 funerals each year, but only one or two marriages or baptisms. We have quite a good balance for which I'm grateful.

Things do inevitably go wrong at times. No matter how many times I checked where the boards were under the

artificial turf around a grave, the one time I didn't was the
one time my left foot disappeared down an eighteen inch
drainage trough behind the head of the grave. Trying to
recover my balance was far easier than attempting to recover
my composure as I committed the departed to 'God's
merciful keeping'.

Another worry in these types of service is the signing of the
registers at a wedding. When everyone begins to relax in the
vestry, now that the public bit is over, then things can go
wrong. It's so easy to marry the best man to the bridegroom
on the official document and it can take some considerable
time to correct the mistake. Although it hasn't happened yet
I'm sure there will be a first time. Richard is very tolerant of
my mistakes. He has to be for his own sanity.

I first fully understood the phrase, 'an Englishman's home
is his castle' in February 1985. Our 1984 Christmas present
finally arrived on January 11th, 1985 when the removal firm
brought our well packed belongings out of storage and
delivered them to our designated house. For six months we
had lived in a single room in a parishioner's house, as the
house we were to be given was not acquired in time for our
arrival. With only what we could transport in our car
Pauline, our hamster and I weathered the trials and tribu-
lations of the house buying process. I can't say we enjoyed it
a great deal, but the lady we stayed with did all in her power
to ease the situation and she and her family could not have
been more hospitable. We felt gratitude to her for putting up
with us and yet deep frustration as the situation refused to
budge. Deadlines came and went and with them our spirits
dwindled. I kept reminding myself that ministers rely on
other people's charity for their material possessions and that
this was a good thing to learn, but my emotions constantly
got the better of me and I realised I was beginning to feel
bitter. Almost inevitably this bitterness was directed towards those responsible for buying the house, as it sometimes seemed that they were unaware of the urgency of the
situation. This was a particular difficulty for Pauline, having
left behind a home and full-time job, and longing to settle

fully into the new area. Difficult for me too, starting a job with few books and no study, and sometimes feeling that I was failing to provide properly for my family. When Christmas finally came and we opened the tea chests full of our things we rejoiced, pulled up our drawbridge and immediately forgot what it was like to have been in the situation at all.

Most important in choosing a curacy is deciding whether one can work with the vicar. When I came to Reigate there were two ministers already here, each with six years experience of the parish. Richard Thomson, with his twenty years of experience in the ministry had previously been in Hull, Croydon, Shoreditch and Vevey in Switzerland. George Lings had been in Harold Wood and was serving an extended second curacy in Reigate. As well as this Mike Fox, Tim Sterry, and Kenneth Habershon, all ordained, were honorary curates with specialist skills which they used in and around the area. The then Bishop of Kingston, Keith Sutton, interviewed me shortly before ordination. Recognising that there was not only a plethora of clergy, but an astonishing wealth of talent and skill among the laity, he advised me to, 'Keep your eyes open, listen to what people say and learn.' In fact I was largely dumb-struck and goggle-eyed as the curtain went up. The standards were very high, almost too high and I felt inadequacy tinged with challenge.

Leading worship and being involved musically were two of my strengths. I had enjoyed the 'buzz' of performing in front of large crowds of people from music college days. Singing or playing before thousands of people at times, never really worried me. It was the high standards of other areas of ministry, especially preaching, that concerned me. I had vowed in college not to make my mind up conclusively about doctrinal issues such as divorce, remarriage, or homosexuality until I had some practical experience of talking to people involved with these situations. College had been very clinical, and although it had given me some of the tools of theology it hadn't really prepared me to minister to real people. I don't particularly blame college for that, but I do regret not having the tools to understand myself. Suddenly I found myself feeling things I'd never felt before – responsibility, accountability, expectations of 'holy' behaviour and total knowledge of the Bible, to name but a few. It was a time of enormous internal upheaval. I had expected to be giving out, to be ministering to others, to be employing my skills in the service of the body of Christ. I actually found that I hardly knew myself at all. In a homegroup I shared my concerns and the group almost fell apart. It was only the skills of the leaders that helped me understand that my honesty could be threatening. At my Selection Conference one of the selectors had asked me, 'What do you most need in order to minister to others?' I had responded instinctively, surprising myself, 'Privacy'. I now had to fight for it and I resented that. I know now that I am quite a contemplative person. I prefer to be on my own. If I'm with a large group of people I must have a function, preferably as part of a team. I'm not good at being consistent and working towards long term goals. I was unnecessarily hurt by the parishioner who said to me quite factually, not meaning any offence, that she had been in the parish for fifty years and I would only be there for five. I accept that perspective now and can work with it. I'm a project orientated person and the projects need to be short, a year or eighteen months at the most. Before I knew that, I felt enormous inner failure when a music group I had set up only lasted for fifteen months. We wrote and recorded an album, as well as engaging in many concerts before it died, but my initial expectation was that it should continue for much longer.

Both Pauline and I searched for somewhere to be ourselves for some time before we were forced by private circumstances to face up to our relationship. When we became engaged in 1979 she told me she had always wanted to marry a vicar. I'm not sure I'll ever become one or whether she still feels the same, but I was pleased at the time. When we arrived in Reigate with only a few belongings and our hamster we decided it would be nice to start a family when we took up residence in our house. For six months we lived with this thought. It was to be another four and a half years before Helen arrived. Waiting doesn't come easily to either of us, less so when we're in the public eye. We kept the whole thing as quiet as possible in the parish. I just couldn't bear it if people knew, but people would joke unknowingly about our not having children. 'One day you'll succumb to the pressures and start a family,' as though we were resisting it. Certainly, in an area where success is expected we began to feel more and more inadequate. The consultant at the infertility clinic, a member of the church family, seeing the depth of our depression commented that we should seek counselling help – which we did, out of the parish.

Looking back on that period it's hard to remember the emotional struggle we went through, the challenge to our sexuality, the inadequacy, and my fear of taking baptisms. People said the kindest things at times, but sympathy is as far from empathy as the east is from the west. With Helen now over a year old and another baby on the way, it's difficult to remember the pain of that time. I do remember the area bishop being helpful, his concern for us was deeply touching. It annoyed us when people said that even though it was hard we would be able to minister to others when we'd come through it. 'Blow them,' I thought, 'it's us I'm concerned about.' If we are ever called upon to minister to other childless couples then I would see that as purely secondary to what we learnt about each other. It enriched us, helped us to realise who we are, and why we married each other. To think God put us through the experience in order that we might function better in the ministry gives a very distorted view of him.

It was typical of Richard, the parish and the area, that we were interviewed for the curacy with another couple on the same weekend. Some have said that ministers should not be in competition with each other when seeking God's will and that this kind of competitive interview is all wrong. I quite enjoyed it, but then perhaps that's why this was the right place for me.

When I was appointed Richard went to great pains to protect me from over enthusiastic parishioners trying to grab me for this activity or that. He told me that for six months I was to refer every offer to him for vetting. Most of the time this worked well and gave me an invaluable opportunity to watch, listen and observe various groups functioning. It taught me that one must be selective and on many occasions reply with a gracious 'no'.

Gradually Richard let me get on with things. His method was to ask me to perform a task in his way then allow me the freedom to do it in my way. It might seem a strange technique in an educationally progressive society, but I found it built up trust between us and gave me an insight into his ministry. By the second year of our relationship I realised that Richard was increasingly becoming a friend. We enjoyed each other's company on the occasions we left the parish for an engagement elsewhere. George Lings left and before Will Donaldson came there was a brief time when Richard and I were on our own. This was helpful to me as I was able to share my aspirations for the next twelve months and with Richard's approval I experienced a new freedom while he spent time helping Will to settle in. It seems to me that one of Richard's greatest gifts is clearing the way for others to grow and shine. Once we began to trust each other he always encouraged me to step out and 'have a go'. Very rarely, if ever, did he appear to feel threatened by me.

Richard is by nature a prayerful person and by and large his decision making is based on a disciplined life of prayer and Bible study. As one trained as a professional soldier and officer he can come across as a commander of men rather than a tender of souls. Friends of his have joked affectionately and parishioners have sometimes criticised him unjustly, but as his friend and curate I've had the privilege of seeing behind this exterior into his inner understandings. Richard lives a private life of passionate faith and gracious heartfelt warmth. I've seen it as my job to help him lead the church in the way he sees fit, and to portray his public image in the way he feels is appropriate. When I think he is wrong, he expects me to say so, just as when I need some advice, he will offer it. Richard is one of the few people I have had this valuable kind of relationship with and the fact that I will stay seven years in all bears tribute to that.

One's relationship with a vicar depends also on loyalty and this is a testing experience. I have come up against those who find Richard's style hard to live with, who feel their personalities are ignored. Of course, the curate is the perfect sounding board for these gripes. Parishioners can be unfair to curates in this way. I can't say with my hand on my heart that I've always been totally loyal. I've been tempted and fallen, but it's the only way to learn.

Another area of importance in our relationship is theology and spirituality. We are quite different theologically and somewhat the same spiritually. Yet neither has come between us. Richard is quite conservative theologically and I am more radical. I suppose every curate thinks that, but with my catholic background and my more recent training I detect a less conservative trend in me. I enjoy considering anglo-catholic, pentecostal or other opinions more readily. Spiritually, we both find a musical event like Prom Praise to our liking. I certainly enjoy the challenge of new kinds of spirituality but shy away from huge, evangelical conferences as Richard does. We don't have a regular prayer time together but we both commune with God each day in our own private ways.

Pauline and I have always found it difficult to have a quiet time together. This used to concern us, until we gave up feeling guilty. Now we're exploring again how we can relate spiritually together, given that our backgrounds are different and there's no special magic formula of how it should be done. We feel it is important to be together before God in some way but reading notes and having a prayer time has not worked for us. So it's back to the drawing board.

When I work it out I realise I will have spent almost twenty per cent of my time in the ministry with Richard. The same applies for him, and I know he's been a great influence, so much so that some parishioners see us as always saying the same thing. Although I am by no means a military person and the 'forces' would be the last job open to me, I've enjoyed working with Richard and am glad that I made the decision to come here. Richard is a godly man and I respect him for that and for having the courage of his convictions. He has taught me more than he will ever know. In an age when curacies seem to be three or four years progressing immediately to a daughter church or living I would like to make an appeal for longer curacies, especially among bigger churches where there needs to be more stability. I believe that there is great value in staying for five years or longer. One's philosophy of ministry becomes more established and the credibility of the minister becomes more effective. It took two years to become known, two years to become established and then three years to achieve something, in my case a new leadership structure, which is only half finished at the moment.

Richard did let me get on with things. He allowed me to research and implement a new leadership pattern in the church, one allowing more shared leadership. But Pauline and I have been a part of many things. We began as members of a homegroup with no responsibility for its running. This is part of the philosophy of the church for its ministers. We were also assigned two lay pastors who were there to counsel and generally befriend us. We met each month and shared all our frustrations and problems. These pastors have not always been the same people but have always been members of the church and a source of relief from the pressures of church work. They have also encouraged Pauline and me to share our mutual feelings concerned with ministry. We spent a year in the baptism preparation class and then a year in the marriage preparation class. For a time we led the 18–23 group and then Spearhead, the 14–18 group. Early on, I began a group for men and women thinking of ordination. This has continued in various forms to support the fifteen or so people who are at the differing stages of their journey towards the full-time ministry. Recently I have started some 'Christians in business' groups. In an area where there are many professional men and women seeking to bring a Christian attitude to their work environment it has been a great joy to hear them expressing their views and seriously thinking through the implications of their jobs.

The most significant course I've been on was organised by POT (post ordination training) and was located at the Maudsley Psychiatric Hospital in South London. I was placed on an anorexic ward having spent a whole two hours being prepared! As I sat in the common room among the twelve general psychiatric patients and the twelve anorexic patients, I once again felt the dig of the clerical collar in my chin. It was about twenty minutes before a brave soul came up to me and sat beside me. Casually he leaned over to me and gently whispered in my ear, 'What are you in here for then?' Thus began a profound experience which has remained with me in vivid detail and I imagine will shape my thinking about pastoral care for some time.

Being a true North Easterner I have needed to adjust to the South East. The pace of life is so frantic, the choices are so wide, that even the smallest of decisions takes careful thought. I guess this all took its toll on me in November 1988 when I began to feel very tired and stale with my work. By January I found myself very unhappy and depressed. Depression is one of those horrible diseases that creeps up without our noticing until it's too late. Through January and February I was less than useless at home and at work. I remained in bed quite a lot of the time trying to keep up an impression of work by attending the occasional meeting but I knew deep inside that things were far from right. I developed pains in my side which were a mystery to my doctor except that he reckoned I was under stress. March 5th came and Helen was to be dedicated, a joyous day with lots of friends invited for lunch and tea. By two in the afternoon I was lying on my bed watching TV whilst the crowd downstairs

wondered where I was. Eventually one of our guests, a
psychotherapist called Dr Andy Stanway, came and found
me and the recovery began. I don't know what I would have
done if Andy had not helped me at that time but I was again
very grateful to God for leading him to me.

When I first came here I felt guilty talking to friends from
the inner city churches. 'Leafy Surrey, that's a very cushy
number,' they would say. After some time I began to realise
that although many of the social problems of the inner city
were absent from the area, they were replaced by others just
as difficult. Highly stimulated people can suffer from a
boring home life which drives them on to find other compen-
sating stimulants. The addiction to alcohol, drugs, tranquil-
lisers, lies just below the surface of many people's lives and
can easily make up for hard work and long hours. Although I
have not had a great deal to do with the deliverance ministry
in the area, I know there to be some very acute occult
problems involving horrific spiritual and mental damage.
There is also pressure for perfection. If someone works from
six in the morning until eight at night, travelling in crowded
commuter trains, performing a stressful job, then they are
not likely to be drawn out in the evening to a church meeting
unless it is of the highest standard, well organised and
beneficial. This often seems to result in unhelpful perfection-
ism which deskills everyone and reduces real, honest growth.
The high degree of choice brought about by increasing
wealth makes it simple to change allegiance if a perceived
standard is lowered. It is all too easy to apply this to church
life too and find another church if this one doesn't preach the
right gospel. Pauline found teaching in a private school,
where parents could make certain demands regardless of
what was professionally in the child's best interests, to be
frustrating at times. The child might be removed along with
the fees and placed in another school. This kind of choice
seems to carry the danger of a distrust of any in authority
who disagree, regardless of their expertise. A minister's job is
often to try to disentangle consumerism from commitment
and enable people to be released to find their true selves.

It wasn't long after we moved in that we began to find this consumerism affecting us. We began to acquire the same sort of things as everyone else: a golden retriever, a dishwasher, a video. We had to ask ourselves the question 'Were we becoming materialistic?' I realise now that there is a part of me that enjoys home comforts. I hate living frugally. I drive a Golf GTI, my wife a Volvo bought out of a legacy. We still live without being able to save, but we make sure we go on an exciting holiday each year. It's essential for us to get away regularly and often. Life in the ministry is pressurised, but we're only human and there need to be compensations. A minister who tries to become a martyr by devoting him or herself to the job completely becomes just that, a martyr, leaving a wife and children wondering whether that was really God's will.

Pauline and I made a pact when we first married that every eighteen months or so we would seek marriage guidance counselling to keep track of our relationship, and in 1987 we found ourselves at a marriage renewal day set up by the diocese. It set me thinking about the psychology of vocation. Sometimes the pull towards the ministry is stronger than the attraction of marriage. Hence the ministry widows and widowers. I too felt this strong pull to the ministry until the day I looked in my diary and saw that at 11.30 p.m. I was to see a lady in the parish called Pauline Dodds! A cruel but effective reminder that spouses are often the last people who receive our attention. It's a problem that won't go away and when children come along the goalposts get moved constantly. However, I still believe that I'd rather leave the ministry tomorrow than marry the job.

I do not in fact see myself in parochial ministry in the immediate future. I am too project-centred and in need of using my specialism, to be able to withstand the generality of parish life on my own. I enjoy it now because I'm not in charge and I'm working with a team. Garth Hewitt came to us some three years ago and said that there are general ministers called to specific areas and specific ministers called to general areas. I found that helpful to understand where I am at. I think I'm one of the latter but as yet I haven't discovered what I am to do next.

There are all sorts of possibilities in the ministry ranging from the bread and butter of parochial work, working on the front line, to jobs hidden away in Church House which are equally crucial but rarely seen by the person in the pew. In 1988 I attended a Dale Carnegie management course and discovered that there is a lot that the church can learn from secular business. I don't think that business methods can simply be imposed onto church organisations but certainly some of the techniques could be very useful. Perhaps that is an area for me to explore. The influence of some in-depth counselling added to the experience at the Maudsley Hospital has made me consider a future role in pastoral care. By the end of 1989 I shall have been to America three times to study and research lay ministry. The USA is an exciting place for me. I wonder whether we might study and work there for a time before coming back to the church here with new insights. While here in Reigate I have been involved in the setting up of NEAC 3 and the annual AEA conferences. I've also been active in the bishop's liturgical committee, and more recently I was appointed a lecturer and tutor at the school for Lay Readers in the diocese. These experiences have given me a desire to see change in the Church of England appropriate to our ever deepening understanding of God. Whether in the area of vocation and ministry, or in training, I am drawn to serve God and use my skills to enable others. When the time comes to leave here I shall weigh up the opportunities. People ask what the ministry is like, and I can only reply that it is unique. I am not a manager of a business, I am not an administrator. I am neither a psycho-therapist, nor a social worker. I am not a great orator and certainly not a mystic and yet being involved in a parish means knowing a little about all these disciplines. On the other hand I could take any one of these areas and probably find a niche somewhere that would allow me to concentrate on it. Although the full time ordained ministry does challenge the very heart of a person's life emotionally, physically, mentally and above all spiritually, it is an exciting job. Trying to live comfortably with the dog collar means coming to heel in all the above areas, which can be a painful and slow process. It's not something that can be taken lightly, but there are compensations and as I look back and then forward, I realise I'm certainly enjoying it.

Graham Dodds is a curate at St Mary's Reigate, Surrey.

Chapter Three

GOING UP THE CANDLE

by

Stephen Leeke

He deserves to be preached to death by wild curates

Sydney Smith

It was a day or two before Christmas and the house was in chaos. My wife, Margaret was baking so there were tins and flour and mincemeat jars everywhere in the kitchen as well as the inevitable loads of washing. Our young children were playing, so cars and Lego and toy boxes littered the floor. In the middle of all this I was engrossed in Christmas wrapping paper when the doorbell rang.

It was the vicar of a nearby Cambridge parish whom I had first met three months before when on a student pastoral placement – that's a few weeks spent helping in a parish to pick up a few tips – and here he was standing totally unexpectedly on the doorstep of the shambles I called home. I didn't know what to say so I stood with my mouth open as he spoke.

'I hope it's not inconvenient but the bishop had mentioned that you were looking for a curacy and I'm looking for a curate.'

'Yyyes, I . . . I . . . I . . . You . . . You . . . You'd better come in.'

So he and I sat in the hubbub of spin-driers and children to chat. I knew, from the little 'Situations Vacant' letters that all the theological colleges get (and final year students search through) that there was a vacancy for a lady in this anglo-catholic parish. But the conversation, which seemed to carry on without me, also seemed to assume that I would be offered the job. I reminded him that I was an evangelical male and that I could only preach and teach what I believed, but he made it plain that although it was very bad taste even to mention it, he was sure there would be no difficulty. After half an hour of chatting, we said goodbye and he tootled off on his rattling bike.

I had just been interviewed for a job without any warning, surrounded by the kids, in my old clothes, at home! Thank goodness my previous experiences of clergy interviews had prepared me for this laid-back approach.

As we debriefed, Margaret and I reminded ourselves that the parish had a high-church tradition and that I was considered unacceptably low-church by some of my fellow Ridley students. Yet he was very friendly, we got on well together, and I was getting desperate!

Our problem was . . . too many children!

Although many of the older vicarages seem to have been designed for families of at least ten, our six children had persistently proved to be my biggest challenge. I shall always remember the day the Diocesan Director of Ordinands (DDO) called to say that although they thought I would probably make a good parson they couldn't send me to a Selection Conference because if I were recommended they wouldn't be able to support my large family while I was training. It was a real body blow to us early in the process, to find that money was the deciding factor. I shall always be grateful to God and my home church that they had the generosity to make up the shortfall in finances (a four figure sum) so that we could proceed. I did one year on the East Anglian part-time study course and a year full-time at Ridley Hall.

The C. of E. seems to believe, against all the evidence, that a curate is a young man of about 23 with no attachments. So most curate's houses are small. When I applied for curacies I was told a number of times, 'We'd love to have you but we don't have the accommodation your family needs.' This was a bit depressing and forced us to widen our net.

The same question had raised its ugly head at the Selection Conference, a three day long interview, usually referred to as an ACCM (it rhymes with smack 'em). Some people have sneaked into the army by lying about their age, and one of my brothers did the same thing in order to give blood while under-aged. I hid the truth about our sixth child. I confess. I told the truth when I filled in the form, we did only have five then. But by the time the conference came there were six. I dared not tell anyone there for fear they'd turn me down on that count alone. I wouldn't have minded being turned down. In fact it would have been a great relief. But to be turned down on the basis of our fertility would have been too embarrassing to take. Of course if they'd asked: 'Only five?' I would have told the truth but it didn't come up so I kept mum.

The whole process of being ACCMed is a bit daunting and some of the chaps there, they were all literally 'chaps', were quite worked up about it. They were keen to get through, or in one case his wife was. He made a phone call home before and after each interview to discuss strategy. That problem is one good argument for the ordination of women! But I was much more relaxed. I really didn't mind. I could take it or leave it. I had doubts about whether clergy were on the whole a good thing and I had a sort of feeling that if the church was silly enough to let someone like me be a minister, I didn't want to be a part of it!

On the second morning of the conference the readings at the service were about the awesome power of God. Somehow the pouring rain added to the slightly oppressive atmosphere. I was still pondering some of these ideas as I paid a visit to the gents. The chaps in the lounge playing snooker saw an enormous flash and a very loud bang as a lump of lightning buried itself in the lawn outside. In the confines of the smallest room I thought the Lord had decided to punish my arrogance in daring to offer my hopelessly inadequate life. The whole tiny room seemed to shake as the enormous roar reverberated around it. My eyes were dazzled, my ears were deafened, my legs jerked with fear and the seat rattled in time with my racing heart. I honestly thought it was curtains for me. Eventually I realised that I was still alive and life had to go on, though it could never be the same. I tried my best to summon a casual appearance and sauntered lamely back to the snooker.

'Are you all right?' someone asked.

'Yes, fine. Did anyone hear a bang?' I answered in a matter of fact way, wondering whether it was internal or external to my person . . .

'It must have been a thunderbolt,' the youngest chap said and pointed to where it landed; 'just outside the loos.'

'I was in there,' I said in an anguished voice. And with as much sympathy as you can expect from people at a three day interview they burst out laughing.

The first actual man to man interview that day was with a famous clergyman who had responsibility for 'testing our vocation'. Were we really called by God – or at least did we really believe we were? I didn't have a hope and I knew it. I knocked and a voice said, 'Enter.'

But there seemed to be nobody in the room. I was beginning to worry about my sanity when a voice said, 'Sit down, make yourself comfortable, I have!'

He was lying full length on the sofa, shoes off, hands behind his head, eyes virtually closed. I sat down opposite his head. Not exactly comfortable.

'You've got a bit of a sense of humour,' he said.

So has God, I thought.

But I said, 'I have?'

'On the form it asks: What have you to offer the Church of England?' (That's a trick question.) 'And you've answered that you are sure that the God who spoke through Balaam's ass can use you.'

'I did? Oh! yes. Umm. Well . . .'

'Humour doesn't usually work in these circumstances but you've got away with it! . . . Why do you think God is calling you?'

'The people in my church said . . . The vicar . . .' None of it very convincing stuff.

The interview ended with my celebrated interviewer

asking the forty-four thousand dollar question straight out. 'Do you want to be ordained?'

Before I could answer, my voice said, 'Yes!'

I left him, still with eyes closed, hands behind head, flat-out on the sofa.

You could have knocked me over with a postage stamp when the bishop's letter a week later said that I had been recommended for training. I wouldn't have been surprised if they'd recommended me for treatment!

One parish we visited about a year later for a Sunday 'look-see' and interview was a delightful large seaside parish with a huge town centre church. After attending the rather formal sung matins we went for dinner with the vicar and his wife and discussed the usual churchy things. After the meal we retired to the beautifully furnished sitting room and the conversation came round to music, which my wife loves, and all seemed well until I said:

'By the way, I can't sing.'

The room fell silent. The vicar looked in the other direction. His wife smiled pityingly. And I knew that this was one of those cases when you say, 'Although it was a most interesting parish and we were made very welcome and it would be a joy to work there, we couldn't help feeling that it was not right for us.' The vicar agreed!

By the December of my final year most of the students were fixed up. I was still looking, so the college principal contacted my bishop to ask him if he could find anywhere for me to work. The bishop who has sponsored you feels some responsibility for finding you a job and so mine thought of this nearby parish (which needed a woman but might accept a man with a ready made Sunday school) mainly because we wouldn't even have to leave our present house. Hence the sudden appearance of Chris on the yuletide doorstep. And our visit the next Sunday to his church.

One of the irrational rules of the 'Find the Curacy' game is: 'You mustn't tell anyone why you have come.' That's not easy with six kids. When a whole pew is suddenly commandeered by a large and vociferous family, people tend to wonder why. And, who? where from? how long? what next? and is it an answer to prayer or a punishment for something? But it was quite a culture shock for my family.

They were used to lively student congregations lapping up thirty minute sermons. Here it was over before we had settled down. We had a music group of guitars, flutes, violins and so on. Here they had a robed choir, half of them little children whose mouths didn't synchronise with the words. We were used to clergy in black and white robes. Chris wore what one of the family described as a carpet. And there was a sort of candle dance before the Gospel was read and a migration of Mosaic proportions to the font at the back of the church for the baptism. There were servers everywhere, all sorts of strange movements, and bowing, bell ringing and cross making. There almost seemed to be more people in robes of one sort or another than there were in civvies, and about seventy or eighty people in all. I think Margaret and the children wondered what had hit them, but I had been prepared by my pastoral placement.

My very first visit to this church had been quite an experience. I went to a 6.30 evensong in July and arrived less than five minutes early. There was a bicycle parked in the porch and the bells rang out cheerfully. I anticipated a bustle of about 50 people probably mainly young marrieds, judging by the parish. The beautiful medieval church was almost empty, half a dozen virile 20–30 year olds pulled at the bell ropes enthusiastically and at the opposite end a man in a suit moved prayer books beyond the chancel screen. I took a pair of books from the pile by the door and sat in a seat in the middle of the church. I settled myself and knelt to pray for the service. As I opened my inner mouth a voice called out.

'Don't sit there!'

Although I am kneeling, no-one else is sitting so he must mean me, I thought. As I looked up the curate loomed before me wearing a black cassock and the most fulsome beard I have ever seen.

'We meet in the chancel in the evenings,' he said and led me through the screen asking what I was doing there.

To my surprise there were about five other people secreted beyond the screen and I was shown to a vacant stall. The beard asked my name and disappeared through a trapdoor in the wall. One minute later the vicar came through the same hole and welcomed me; then disappeared again. I introduced myself to the lady next to me. Her name was Doris and she proved to be very friendly and helped me, unnecessarily, to find the hymns. The bells stopped ringing and the ringers evaporated.

The vicar had expressed the fear that the organist might not turn up (but he did) and had apologised for the relatively small number of people, as did Doris. I said that it was nice to have a smaller group sometimes.

'What is your normal evening congregation?'

'Up to a hundred,' I replied.

'Oh! That must be your main service.'

'Um, no not exactly.'

'How many do you get in the morning?'

'Two or three hundred, I suppose.'

'Oh – Well it's good to hear of congregations like that,' Doris said.

'I'm sure I shall enjoy a more cosy service which is a little less formal,' I assured her.

The service proved to be very formal. It was straight Prayer Book evensong with sung versicles and responses, psalm, Magnificat, Nunc Dimittis, and four hymns. The prayers were on the theme of the majesty and enormity of God. The lessons were read in the loud clear and enunciated manner one might expect in a cathedral. The notices were read as if no one knew anything about them. There was a strong exhortation to help with the churchyard clearance which many of those present were already involved in, so it must have been very pointed for the one or two who weren't. The sermon on the doctrine of the Trinity explained the objections to be found among Moslems and Jews and the ideas of Thomas Aquinas. It could all have been more relevant! What an introduction!

However, by the end of my two weeks 'helping' in the parish I had learnt a great deal about vicaring and came to quite like this, to me, very different church fellowship and their friendly vicar.

So when I was offered the job, after praying about it and after squaring it with Margaret and the mob, I took it.

I had two competing worries:

1. I shall be changed into a card carrying anglo-catholic. This was known in Ridley and elsewhere as 'Going up the candle.'

2. I will find it impossible to fit into this set up. Like a size ten foot in a size six shoe!

I needed some sort of assurance that I was not going to be either swallowed up or spat out! It came in a most unusual way.

On my next appointment with Chris I had to search the churchyard for him. I was later to spend much of my curacy doing this. Before I found him I got my foot stuck in the loose mud left near a recently filled grave. As I wiped the worst of that awful clay-like soil off my recently polished shoe, I noticed some tree roots which had been cut by the grave-digger and thrown on one side. Two roots had crossed each other at right angles as they grew and had fused themselves together. Here lying in my path was a natural, simple, rugged cross. It was a powerful symbol to me that God was with me in this next big step, even if I *was* likely to put my foot in it sometimes. I took it home, cleaned it up, varnished it and it hangs over the desk as I write now. It is a constant reminder to me that God is at work, often under the surface.

Most of my actual ordination as a deacon is no more than a hazy recollection. But there was a moving service in Ely Cathedral which came after three days of quiet retreat. I have a photo of myself and the eleven others with the bishop after the service, and a signed and sealed document to prove that it really did happen. That same Sunday evening I read to the tiny evensong congregation a long statement that assured them that I assented to the Thirty-nine Articles and would only use services which were allowed. Witnessed by the churchwardens, I signed the pledge and started a new role as curate.

The more perceptive readers will have realised that mine was an unusual route to the cloth. It is rare for someone to get away with selection, training (on a course and at a college), and beginning a full-time curacy without moving more than a mile. But it does have advantages.

The first person I was asked to visit as a parson, was a lady who was in hospital for a small operation on her leg veins. I already knew her, as her son was a long-standing friend from teenage days, though I hadn't seen him for years. It was a great privilege to pray with these old friends in a new relationship. She was pleased to see me and her thoughts were quickly transferred from the antiseptic hospital ward to the bustling family home and memories of her son's wide circle of friends. I was to learn that much of the value of hospital visits is in the change of mental scenery one can bring or evoke.

Unfortunately the treatment did not go well and a couple of weeks later I had to help this lady and her family to come to terms with the fact that her leg had to be amputated. This was of course a very traumatic time for her and I felt it acutely. What can you say to someone who went into hospital for a minor op and within a few days was facing life in a wheelchair?

I shall never forget the shock of that occasion, my faltering attempts to pray with her, and the time I spent alone at home afterwards coming to terms with the experience. But it was a joy to see her face the facts bravely and slowly accept the limitations of her new life. Her delightful bungalow was modified and her husband was domesticated. Her interest in the garden returned and a friendship with two of our children developed. They called to see her regularly after school and she told them all that the nesting blackbirds had been doing, showed them her needlework, and so on.

Just when things seemed to be settling down, her husband became ill and soon died. It was another body blow to this small and wounded lady. She fought on and with the help of a whole circle of friends that she had cultivated, many of them church members, she was soon coping again. I could hardly believe my eyes when I saw the cheerful postcard she sent to the children from Edinburgh after she bravely joined a holiday arranged for disabled people. Just before I left the parish at the end of my curacy she proudly told me that her son, my long standing friend, had been appointed to a Baptist pastorate in a village near his home in Wales. I was surprised and amazed at the secret things God was doing in the lives of people I knew and how faith can grow through troubles.

One of the main things about a curacy is the relationship with your vicar. Some vicars are too possessive and some are jealous; some are unable to share their job and others expect the curate to do everything; one may be secretive while another can't keep a confidence.

My vicar was very easy to get on with. He seemed able to accept my idiosyncracies, ignorance, chaotic lifestyle and cheeky sense of humour without being upset. A sort of rapport developed between us that allowed us occasionally to spice our sermons with the odd friendly jibe at our partner. In fact it was not unusual for one to interrupt the other with a quip or comment and this kind of knock-about humour added real fun to the experience of learning together for the whole church. It is a great credit to Chris that he was able to accept this side of me, and made me feel quite at home in this different church. But I had no idea that this would happen when we met for our first staff meeting. We got round to discussing who would preach, and Chris said in a matter of fact way,

'I don't want you to use notes for your sermons. You

can have notes of course, but I don't want you to look at them.'

This was a bombshell. At college we had been encouraged to write out the sermon in full. We had Monday sermon classes where we would dissect the sermon that one of us preached on Sunday and comment on the main areas: Theological content, Aim, Structure, Opening, Ending, Appropriate choice of words, Was it on the right wavelength? Were there good illustrations? Did it have a clear application? Was it powerful enough?

As if that were not enough we had to analyse the preacher: Was his voice strong enough? or too strong? Did he use appropriate gestures? Did he establish eye contact? Any distracting mannerisms? Did he create a good impression? You can imagine the effect that Monday's impending inquisition had on Sunday's preacher! Semi-paralysis!

I quickly found that I hated reading sermons word for word and preferred a skeleton of notes to which I could add the details I planned. But the boss, my new vicar, was saying;

'Nothing, just memory.'

I looked at his face. No there was no tell-tale smile; he meant it. No notes.

He sensed my incredulity, and said;

'I know it sounds hard but I've found from experience that it makes it easier to listen to, and if you can't remember what you want to say then the people probably won't remember what you said either!'

My first sermon there felt a bit like free-fall parachuting. It feels dangerous and needs great courage, but it is exhilarating, there's an enormous sense of freedom, if you land safely there is a marvellous feeling of achievement, and for the congregation it is interesting to watch!

Needless to say after these regular leaps of faith I soon felt able to do informal assemblies, off-the-cuff talks and emergency Sunday school lessons without a worry. It was learning to swim by the 'in at the deep end' method and it worked for me! I know all my college contemporaries were horrified. They were sure that heresies, embarrassing silences or empty padding were bound to creep in. They were probably the very things that were missed out!

Another item of business at that first staff meeting was a funeral. In two days time there was to be a funeral at the local crematorium and Chris wanted me to do it.

'But I've never done one before,' I said.

Chris smiled and said, 'You've just come out of college and probably know more about it than I do. No one ever taught me how to do it. You'll be all right.'

I put my foot down here, or rather, I pleaded with him.

'You do this one and I'll come along and watch, then I'll do the next.'

He gave in, but didn't feel he had anything to offer as training in this area of ministry. Again, I was fortunate because I had been to this particular crematorium as part of the course: they'd shown us round, explained the process and which button to push to draw the curtains round the coffin at the end of the service. We had also done mock funerals, but I still cringe when I remember the video recording of my attempt. The recording of another student's effort became an item of entertainment which was watched over and over again by groups of staff and students who invariably ended up in tears of laughter as he pulled at the heart strings of the imagined friends of the 7-year-old deceased, saying, 'Johnny won't be coming out to play any more.' And, 'There will be a spare bottle in the school milk crate . . .'

When the time came for the real funeral I joined the mourners and watched how it was done. I learnt a great deal at that service and was able to develop a style very similar to Chris's. I separated an obituary about the person, at the beginning of the service, from a very short but appropriate explanation of the Bible reading chosen for the funeral. It helped avoid the suggestion that their good deeds secured them a place in heaven, or that I imagined that everyone I buried was a saint.

I was also introduced to the crematorium manager. They

seem to have a simple approach to clergy. There are two
sorts: those who can do a funeral in less than the thirty
minutes allowed; and waffling incompetents. That particular manager still smiles when I go, so I must be in the first
group.

Within a month of my ordination Chris was off on holiday
and I was left in charge. This was an awesome responsibility
for me so soon after starting out in this very different job,
although I did have a few retired priests I could refer to for
help with services and the other local clergy. I went as usual
to open the church and say Morning Prayer at 7.30 and
Evening Prayer at 6.00. At one of these lone evening visits I
noticed a plain brown cardboard box about the size of a
shoebox on the table by the door. I looked to see what was in
it, but it was empty. It puzzled me a bit and I moaned to
myself about the way people leave litter as I took it to the
dustbin. When I returned I saw a little piece of paper on the
floor. It might have fallen from the box. I picked it up and
read it:

'Dear vicar,

'It was my father's dearest wish that when he died his
ashes should be scattered in the churchyard of the village he
loved. He died three years ago and we have kept them until
we were able to return to England and to ask you to do this
for us. Unfortunately you were out when we called and we
have to return to Germany today so we had to leave them for
you . . .'

Suddenly it all dawned on me. The box must have held an
urn containing the ashes. But it was empty when I found it!
All sorts of people visited our church. It was not far from a
mental hospital, school children occasionally came in, it was
not unusual to see a complete stranger pop in to pray. But
surely no one would steal an urn full of ashes. I searched
the church. Perhaps someone had put it away somewhere.
Finally I noticed an unusual pile under the back pew. There
was a cigarette stub, an empty whisky bottle and a small
heap of grey ashes just like those they had shown me on my
college trip to the crematorium. What on earth was I going

to do? This was a most objectionable form of sacrilege. I suppose one of those drunks whom I had occasionally seen in the churchyard was so intoxicated that he was willing to steal the very container of this stranger's last remains.

I fetched a dustpan and brush and swept up the ashes. I took them out into the churchyard and with a prayer and a verse from scripture I scattered the ashes on the ground; '. . . earth to earth, ashes to ashes, dust to dust . . .' With another prayer for the poor alcoholic who had plumbed the very depths, I went home hoping I had done the best I could.

On his return from holiday I reported the incident to the boss. He didn't seem as surprised as I was and frowned at me saying 'Didn't you realise you are not allowed to scatter ashes in a churchyard?'

You can scatter them at sea, in a field, a waterfall, a back garden, I've even known them to be burnt in the firebox of a steam engine, but you can't scatter them in a churchyard – they have to be buried! And so I learnt another interesting piece of ecclesiastical law ready for the Trivial Pursuit game we call parish ministry. But if church law says you can't scatter them, an even stronger law says you certainly can't gather them up again, so right or wrong what was done was done.

Chris wrote to the lady in Germany telling her that her wishes had been carried out; he didn't mention the fact that it was illegal or the roundabout way in which it happened.

One of the theological challenges that quickly came my way as a curate was 'sick communions'.

As far as I was concerned Holy Communion was a communal event in which people shared the bread and wine as a reminder of Jesus's death for us. But in this parish (as in very many others) they used to save some in a little cupboard in the wall. Then during the week Chris would take this bread and wine to one of a short list of people who were sick so that they were able to 'make their Communion'.

I wasn't at all sure that I believed in this! It suggested a belief in the magic properties of the elements. Chris however had a very mundane approach. To him I think it was like sending wedding cake to people who couldn't get to the wedding but wanted to feel included. His laid-back style enabled me to accept many of the things which I had had misgivings about. He argued not that they were essential but that they helped some people. He didn't use carefully selected scriptures to justify these, to me frightening new practices. He pragmatically allowed me to come to accept some and learn to live with others and work out my own ideas along the way. I did have problems with the fact that one of the ladies I regularly took communion to because she was housebound, occasionally cancelled my visit because she was going on one of her holidays to America!

The ritual side of things was difficult and Chris had to spend a long time explaining basic things which he had been taught at college, or even before, but which we evangelicals didn't need to know! I think there was a session at Ridley called 'Ritual', held during one lunch hour, but I can't be sure!

It was like learning the steps to a solemn new dance and Chris had to teach me where to be when, to keep in time with my partner, to bow at the end and walk out in a straight line and in the right order. I had to learn the etiquette of a new society. And there were his names for the bits and pieces he used for communion: corporal, burse, veil, chasuble, alb, amice, girdle and so on. It was like a different language and to me it smacked of popery or something. The white thing I wore (a white cassock), which he called an alb, I stubbornly referred to as a 'white thing'. He found me a girdle and didn't mind that I preferred to call it a rope. The whole question of liturgical dress was a problem to me and I broke myself in gently by getting stoles made to the simplest pattern possible. They were plain cloth. No crosses, embroidery or anything. I called them 'coloured scarves'. I couldn't see any logical objection to the actual colour although I did feel that it was wrong for clergy to look too much like Christmas trees laden with decorations.

The whole business could have been quite painful for me if it weren't that Chris was gentle, and very tolerant.

Being a parson isn't primarily about services, but about people. My first solo funeral was of an elderly lady I had met before when visiting. I was almost as nervous as the widowed husband who was a very gentle man and totally crushed. He was fortunate in having a daughter who lived nearby and could help him so his material needs would be taken care of. When I visited him after the funeral he seemed to be broken by the experience and as often happens tears flowed when I prayed with him.

He then said, 'I'm not an educated man like you' (little did he know!) 'but I find it hard to understand about God and heaven and things.' As the discussion progressed and as I gained his confidence I found that although he seldom went to church (he sent the missus) he read his Bible frequently. Not only that, but he had also read a number of Christian books and obviously took his deliberations seriously. I was able to persuade him to come along on a Sunday though he was very shy. He joined the church's very successful Tuesday Club, mainly for over 60s, and slowly settled into a new life. When I asked about confirmation he told how he had been prepared as a young man but went down with 'flu on the day the bishop came. Now he felt that he was too sullied by the world to offer himself. So many men carry a burden of guilt which cuts them off from God when it ought to draw them to him for forgiveness.

As we talked in a very simple and 'down to earth' way he saw the truth that he could be forgiven and made clean by Jesus, and knew this was what he most wanted. It was a real joy to me to repeat that preparation sixty years later and to present him to another bishop to affirm his commitment to Christ and God's acceptance of him. It was a double joy to see him regularly taking up his new found seat, at the back of the church, and humbly kneeling at the communion rail. He may have been well into his seventies but he was the first shy lamb of my ministry.

When the time came for me to be ordained priest, people

expected me to be full of excitement and enthusiasm for the opportunity to preside at communion, but it wasn't like that. I enjoyed preaching, I enjoyed the contact with people and the privileges of being a parson but I was quite happy as a deacon. Nevertheless the time came and I was duly ordained in Ely Cathedral. The sun streamed in through the stained glass of the magnificent octagon lights and made coloured pools on the floor. I knelt in one of those pools and committed my life again to God's service and a crowd of priests including my vicar descended on me. As these besurpliced clerics shared with the bishop in laying their hands on me, it went dark and folds of warm soft linen covered me. I felt like a chick being brooded by its mother hen and thought of the Spirit of God who brooded on the waters of creation. I felt welcomed into the fellowship of a loving and safe family, and prayed that I would welcome others to Christ's family. Instead of a commissioning and a sending out, it was more a divine cuddle and a drawing in. I was experiencing God's feminine side.

I was quite happy about the 'stage directions' for the main Parish Communion, because I had assisted as a deacon every week for a year. But I had worries about the 8 o'clock Communion. I asked for some guidance from Chris as to what I was supposed to do, where to stand and so on. This is not a trivial question as people have almost gone to the stake over the question of which side of the holy table the priest should stand. The lady chapel was used for the tiny 8 o'clock services. It was impossible to stand either on the left or right of the altar or behind it so one had to use what the cognoscenti call the eastward position. This was another of the things I didn't believe in and I certainly couldn't do the whole service with my back to the congregation. The day before my first one Chris gave me a sheet of paper. It explained exactly where to stand and which way to face for each stage of the proceedings. I literally performed that service with a prayer book in one hand and this script in the other. I found my way haltingly through the complex mime and later asked him for a prayer book with a built in compass! Within a few weeks I had developed a style natural to me and there were no problems.

Ministry is not only about services but about people. Our suburban village was bisected by a railway line, so there was a level crossing in the middle of the busy High Street. British Rail intended to replace the old fashioned manually operated wooden gates with new automatic half barriers. The village was in uproar, worried that there would be nothing between the children going to or from school and the trains trundling through at full speed except a flashing light and a buzzer, and no way of stopping the trains in the event of an accident on the crossing.

There were protest meetings in which both Chris and myself were involved. I joined the group that went to Parliament to lobby our MP, and local councillors were also heavily involved. They didn't seem to be getting far so they decided to have a demonstration. A local councillor who was also the city's mayor and a very tall man headed up the action which was to be a mass sit down on the crossing in order to stop a Saturday morning train. We set about making placards. When we discussed slogans round the dining table and the need for something short and pithy our family came up with 'Gates not graves', and decided that gravestone-shaped boards would reinforce the message. It was all set for the first of February.

When the day dawned it was cold and wet. Chris had contracted a nasty head cold and had to drop out. He warned me to keep warm and offered me his long funeral cape. So as the procession moved towards the heavily-policed crossing it was led by the mayor, head and shoulders above the rest, and a black caped priest apparently carrying a gravestone. The media could not resist this sort of raw theatre and pictures of us both being removed unceremoniously (but respectfully) from the line appeared on that night's national news.

Eventually full barriers were fitted after negotiation between the various local councils and British Rail. But the event entered the folklore of the village. A community drama project put on a play about the history of the village just after I left and its last scene was a recreation of this show of village solidarity. The new crossing gates came into operation on the day I left the parish and my last act as curate was to lead prayers there for safety and to give thanks for the way people had worked together. The congregation on the road on that warm Sunday afternoon included many of those who had demonstrated, County and City Councillors, the MP and slightly red-faced officials from BR.

I don't suppose anyone was converted through these events. We didn't gain lots of new members. But we did witness God's concern for people, and we did confirm the relevance of the Christian faith to the issues of today. That's all part of a curate's job and I loved it!

Stephen Leeke is vicar of Warboys, Huntingdon, in Cambridgeshire.

Chapter Four

BREAKING STEREOTYPES

by

Elizabeth-Anne Stone

Even when the path is normally open – when there is
nothing to prevent a woman from being a doctor, a lawyer,
a civil servant – there are many obstacles, I believe,
looming on her way

Virginia Woolf

'You must be joking Lord!' This was my initial response to God's call into full-time ministry. At the age of twenty I had mapped out my next few years: after university I would go to teachers' training college, then onto a secondary school to teach religious knowledge. I had always envisaged my twenties as being a time for fun and freedom. How on earth could anyone have fun and freedom within the structures of the Church of England? Where had I gone wrong with God? Why this seeming punishment? All the deaconesses I knew were wonderful, godly women, but they were old! Surely I was too young for a twinset and pearls and flesh-coloured stockings? Wrestling with God's call at this point was tough but it was nothing in comparison with what was to come.

God's call came during Holy Communion at Lee Abbey, a Christian conference centre in North Devon. That night I prayed that if what I felt in my heart was from God then he would confirm it in the next year before I left university.

Although I was unwilling for God's next stage in my life, he was patient and confirmed my call in all sorts of ways. I can distinctly remember three separate occasions when friends from different parts of the country suggested that I seriously consider going into the ministry. How unfair of God to tell my friends too! For the next year God used sermons, books and times alone with him to confirm his will. Eleven days after my final examinations my bishop sent me onto an ACCM Selection Conference. I went with much trepidation in my heart and a trump card in my pocket – my age. I was only 21 years old. The selectors would perhaps say I had potential, but surely not yet ready for training. The conference was an ordeal. I felt intimidated by the other women. Many confirmed my own prejudices against women workers. And they all seemed so unhesitating while I was still looking for a way out!

Shortly, I received a letter from my bishop with his selectors' recommendations. I stood in the kitchen and my heart was pounding. What did the future hold? The letter told me. But I could not believe my eyes! 'We wholeheartedly recommend you for training . . . go straight to college this autumn . . . and because of your theology degree do only two years instead of three . . .' I wanted to cry 'Oh no! Nineveh here I come!' But in my heart I knew I needed to stop fighting God's will for my life, to accept it and to throw myself totally into his work and under his care.

In the years that lay ahead it was to take all my courage to hold onto God's love. It took real faith to believe his promises for me. While I never lost the conviction that he was my loving Father I was to go through a time of seriously doubting his call.

The first intimation that my stereotype of a female minister was hopelessly out of date was when I went on the required summer college placement. I was sent to a church in Sheffield and there I met Adele, a parish worker. Here was a woman full of vitality and colour. Someone who was attractive and who did not apologise for being female. Her home was a real home. Each room reflected her personality and there was a sense that time had been spent on the arrangement of furniture and treasured items. Her Irish lilt enticed you and her smiling eyes welcomed and accepted you. It was easy to discover why the children's work under her leadership was growing and why many people turned to her for counselling. Adele gave me a tremendous role model to follow and my appetite for parish work was well and truly stirred.

However, I quickly discovered that working in a parish had its stresses. I was appointed to a large, growing church on the outskirts of London. They had never had a deaconess before and were not quite sure what to expect. I think they were slightly surprised by my brightly-coloured dresses and love for denims! However, the congregation quickly welcomed me into their hearts and lives. The real problem lay not with the people but with my minister. He was a dynamic and creative leader who had plenty of vision and drive. But he was also a person who struggled with the problem of the place of women within the leadership of the church.

The work itself brought the usual joys and frustrations. The young and old were most fulfilling to work with. Of course there were times when the teenagers would let you down dismally by breaking promises, rules and equipment and you began to wonder 'is it all really worth the effort?' But the next day one of them would usually be on your doorstep with a bunch of flowers apologising. The older people were deeply enriching. They brought great joy to all of us who ran clubs and Bible studies for them. We learnt to listen and care for them. It was two-way traffic.

If I had been just a secular worker it would have been great. But I was not. I felt God had called me to the ministry with all that it meant in terms of spiritual leadership, partnership and equality with fellow ministers in proclaiming the gospel. I did not feel it right to do anything less. I knew I was inexperienced, with much to learn, but I wanted to be what God had called me to be, not what someone else thought I ought to be.

The trouble was, I was too inexperienced to realise that one of the most important things you need to discover at your interview is what sort of colleague your prospective vicar wants – is it a 'support' colleague or a fellow leader? If you end up working for a person who wants you only to be seen and not heard, someone to support his ministry alone rather than to develop your own as well, then you could be in trouble.

It was an uneasy three years during which it became more

and more difficult for me as a woman to undertake a full ministerial role. While I am not a card-carrying feminist it brought home to me the difficulty of persuading some men that women do have worth and in God's eyes are equal with them.

Here is a typical example of what I mean. A young woman in the congregation came to me and told me about the problems which she was experiencing in her marriage. I knew I was out of my depth. I shared her story with my vicar, who instead of being pleased that I had broken down barriers enough to gain her confidence, and affirming my role as a counsellor, said 'Stop being a big sister to her, send her to me.' In retrospect I believe it was right for me to counsel a fellow woman and it was his role to train me if he felt I was inexperienced – which clearly I was.

I also found it very stressful when remarks were continually made about the way I dressed; I cannot be the only female curate who would prefer her womanhood and worth affirmed by comment on her quality of work rather than by funny jokes about the clothes she wore.

Then, some time later, without any warning, I was given three months to find another job and move on. I was shattered. This whole episode and the months that followed were exceedingly painful. On the one hand there was the shock and suddenness of it all and the terrible feeling that I had failed, and on the other hand the natural experience of bereavement, of having to leave a parish and people I loved.

You feel ghastly when this sort of thing happens to you; you can't sleep and anxiety eats away at you. Feelings of failure, rejection and anger sweep over you in huge waves. I began to doubt my whole ministry and calling. If people had known this maybe they would have been surprised because the community work which I was involved in was growing and greatly appreciated. But inside I felt broken. It was my first job and the colleague whom I longed to affirm me in the ordained ministry to which God had called me was unable to. Instead of seeing that he would have had problems with any woman curate whoever she had been I took it all very personally.

The church farewell was hilarious. There were amusing stories and songs. The congregation gave me a superb computerised microwave to improve my erratic eating habits and a 'survival' kit of jokey presents that reminded us all of the years of fun and laughter we had shared together. But because of my brokenness, what I really wanted, more than anything else, was a word of encouragement from my vicar.

Somehow or other I found a new job in the Midlands. But driving up the M1 I felt an emotional wreck. How was I going to start again? Would I be rejected or accepted? I felt I couldn't have given any more of myself to my first job. I had done my best. I was young and inexperienced and had made many mistakes, but I had done my best. But where had that left me? Here I was, alone in a new city, no friends nearby, a new job which I didn't have any incentive or confidence for, and a house to set up by myself.

But our gracious Heavenly Father had healing in his hands and was ready to engulf me with his love. Scripture says . . . 'underneath you are the everlasting arms' of God (Deut 33.27). Although I had tumbled into an abyss I experienced afresh the overwhelming sense of Emmanuel – God with us.

Although praying was difficult at this time I never doubted God's love and provision for me. My new minister and his wife, got the whole story, Kleenex and all! I was immediately affirmed as a female church leader and I put on a competent face. For eighteen months it was a real struggle. Healing came but not quickly or easily. I felt isolated. But they were endlessly patient. They allowed me to rant and rave all the time saying that I must allow God to enter into my anger and brokenness. They often spoke about 'wounded healers' and how God uses people who have been through times of testing to help others. Gradually, I learnt to accept the prayers and counsels of those around me, although it hurt my pride. I was the minister and I should be doing the ministering to others, not vice versa! But still the sense of failure remained with me and I began to contemplate leaving the ministry.

Four months later a friend invited me to go on a silent retreat at Lee Abbey. I went desperately needing to re-discover God's will and redirection for my life thinking that I would probably take up nursing. However, in the silence and beauty of the north Devon coast I began to let go of my resentment and bitterness and in their place came joy and peace.

One morning a member of the pastoral team counselled me. And for the first time since leaving London I began to be able to forgive those who had hurt me. But there was more; I had a deep experience of God forgiving me for the bitterness and anger I had held on to. Realising my own fault in clinging to these negative and destructive emotions was essential if my ministry was to continue to grow. And I had to release them from my anger. That night at the Holy Communion service I rededicated myself to God and I knew it was right to stay in the ministry.

It took a year and a half to settle down truly into my new job. Looking back, although my departure from London was badly handled, the move itself was stimulating. There were many new and complementary experiences in store for me which would broaden my whole perspective on life and ministry. I have, recently, again been encouraged by being promoted to Associate Minister. The church's thinking was that after 6 years in the ministry, I would, had I been a man, have been looking to have my own parish. My new position was their recognition of the limitations placed on women within the present structures of the Anglican Church. They were doing all they could!

As a female deacon in the Church of England, I am unsure of what comes next. At college you train with the men and training is the same. It seems unfair that their choices for jobs will be much wider and probably more interesting than yours. At present I feel very fulfilled as a female minister. But there are moments – like in a Holy Communion service which I have planned and led up to the point of the institutional narrative – that I feel regret at having to hand over to a man to do the priestly bits. On the whole I don't meet with much prejudice although there were two occasions in my first job when on the eve of taking funerals I was phoned up by relatives and informed that they wanted a 'proper' funeral for their loved one and so they preferred that one of my male colleagues should take it. You have to be really gracious, and bite back your words, when arranging for a man to take the funeral of someone you have been visiting for weeks. Wedding services have their problems too.

After I was ordained into the diaconate in 1987 I was free to officiate at weddings. Relations are surprised to see you up the front at the rehearsal and they become very worried in case you do it wrong. This puts unnecessary pressure on you which a man doesn't suffer: you have to be word perfect and somehow better than the men otherwise you feel they may say, 'Well, what do you expect, she's only a woman.'

The best bit of pastoral advice given to me as I went into parish life was to split my daily diary up into three sections and work only two out of the three. This rarely happens in my packed schedule but it's still good advice!

Clearly one of the problems, especially for single clergy, is how to keep some sort of balance in your life. The job eats you up. Being busy is infinitely more attractive than going home to an empty house. I'm pushing thirty, and would love to be married, but at the moment I'm always the bridesmaid but never the bride! Being a minister does not exclude you from the pains of singleness.

However, I deeply believe that it's possible to live a full and complete life as a single person. While it may seem desirable for all of us to have a partner we must never lose sight of the fact that in God's eyes Christians do not need anyone to make them complete – we are already complete in him!

He may give us a partner so that we can experience new

dimensions of love, but I still believe it's possible to be 'complete' as one. After all, we are all answerable to God as individuals and he's promised to be all in all to us. We are made whole through him. Too often single people become obsessed by their singleness and it rules their whole lives. They live, breathe and sleep in hope of marriage. The danger here is that God ceases to be their focal point, and marriage becomes a god in itself. However while we are complete in him, it does not remove the growing ache and pain inside. It seems at the moment that all my friends are streets ahead of me and are on their second and third babies. It's not that you begrudge them a child or that you do not share their joy, but it is a constant reminder of your nappy-less days!

However, it's easy to look at married friends, especially male colleagues, and think 'if only I had someone to go back to at night, life would be so different'. But often you fail to see them struggling with questions of time, money and family commitments. The grass is not always greener on the other side!

Meeting men and going out with them while in the ministry is fraught with problems! Some men struggle with your position of authority in the church; others with your spirituality. If you do meet someone, then it's your turn to struggle – this time with your diary. Being a minister can make you very anti-social because you have few evenings free but on the other hand you can be inundated with church social events, which are rarely relaxing. People still ply you with questions about work, the only difference being that you've got a glass of wine in your hand!

There is something worse! – the unavoidable fan club of social inadequates! I do not mean to seem heartless, but in your most private moments you do wonder if you are not doomed to attract only the 'oddballs' in life! It makes you feel unclean when the only men who give you the eye are those with sexual hang-ups!

At this moment my church is helping me as I face the unwanted attention of a very disturbed young man who taunts me at the church during the day and bangs on my door in the middle of the night, shouting obscenities. Not only does this frighten me but I am embarrassed and concerned for my neighbours. Although he has a record against women, the police, who have been very sympathetic, are unable to do anything until he commits another similar offence!

Holidays are the absolute must if you are to survive the ordained ministry. I love 'backpacking' and for the last four summers have been to some very exciting places abroad with a like-minded fellow female minister. I love being away from the telephone and my filofax, and having the freedom to choose what to do every day. It is great fun too seeing people's expression change when they suddenly realise that the two women with them, who are dressed perhaps only in teeshirts and shorts or a bikini, are actually ordained ministers! It's funny how some people think that ministers are members of a third sex!

Despite the difficulties and stresses of parish life, the delights outweigh the problems. Nothing can surpass the joy of leading someone into a personal faith with Jesus Christ and to helping them grow into a mature disciple. It is endlessly exciting to see God intervene in people's lives in many ways. I feel privileged that God has called me to the ordained ministry: how could I ever have thought it would be a punishment!

If God is calling you, don't look over your shoulder at 'Nineveh', just go for it!

NOTE
This is a true account of the experience of the author whose real name, and those of others concerned, have been withheld.

Chapter Five

SERVING IN THE COUNTRYSIDE

by

Stephen Mourant

Of late years an abundant shower of curates has fallen upon
the north of England

Charlotte Brontë

'Who is on the Lord's side? Who will serve the King? Who will be His helpers, other lives to bring?' was the final hymn at the Baptist Church, St Helier, Jersey, on Sunday February 14th 1971 during which I made an open commitment to Jesus Christ.

My parents, keen Christians and Methodists, had prayed for me faithfully since before I was born; church attendance was part of their lives and our family life, as was grace at mealtimes, the occasional Bible story amongst other children's stories, and prayers for us at night.

For me, making this commitment was accompanied by a sense of peace and a sense of 'coming home', like the Prodigal Son. Although I had never seriously gone astray, as a teenager in my heart and mind were strong intents and desires for sin. It was only the strong and loving discipline of my parents that kept me from 'doing'.

Once I had made that step of receiving Christ, something changed in me; my school reports, which had previously read 'Has no confidence' changed to 'Has far more confidence this term'.

The call to full-time ministry was always at the back of my mind, but I could not see how it would be fulfilled. A friend of mine, Henry Le Ruez, who had been converted some weeks after the 1972 Crusade, had begun work in a local finance company. A few months before I left school, he suggested that I applied for a job there. I was offered a post and worked there for seven years. I enjoyed it immensely. I learned there how important it was not only to talk about my faith but also to live it.

After my commitment to Christ at the Baptist Church, I never returned there to worship but got involved in the Methodist Church. I began preaching on the Methodist circuit as a local preacher on trial, an experience I enjoyed, but one which left me increasingly frustrated. The circuit system meant different preachers each Sunday and there was a complete lack of continuity in sermons and teaching. There was a lack of vision for outreach to those not yet Christians, and within me there was a struggle between what I wanted, and what the Lord wanted. I was wanting to apply to the lives of others what I knew was not true in my own life.

In 1975 I occasionally attended St Paul's Church in St Helier, an evangelical Anglican proprietary chapel. Proprietary chapels are outside the Church of England 'system'. They receive no financial support from the Church Commissioners. Nigel Holmes, the incumbent, was intent on building the church up as a teaching and training centre. I became increasingly drawn to what the Lord was doing there. In the late 1960s, the church had almost closed through lack of members. Under God, Nigel and his wife Anne began a work which built a congregation of around a hundred. Most were converts of the previous five years. After a struggle within myself, I left the Methodist Church I had attended and joined St Paul's in September 1975. For a while I took a back-seat. But soon I was involved in leading and preaching and helping with summer open air meetings in the pedestrian precinct in St Helier, reaching out to holiday-makers.

One sure way to know if God is calling someone to full-time ministry is to start letting him use them where they are. And so during that period, 1975 to 1979, I became involved in almost every aspect of God's work at St Paul's. One friend used to call me the 'honorary curate'! But I had much to learn. I served also on the church council, and was secretary for a year prior to going to College (being PCC secretary certainly teaches you to listen to other people!).

In 1979, after I had experienced what some Christians call 'being broken', one local rector said to me, 'Stephen, have you ever considered the Anglican ministry?' My immediate reply was, 'Yes, and the answer is no!' But that question would not go away. I thought about it for weeks and then, one Sunday afternoon, had a long talk with the man who asked the question, Denis Gurney. (He was in pastoral charge of St Paul's at the time during the long interregnum following Nigel Holme's departure.) All my excuses for not going into the Church of England ministry ('it would be like a strait-jacket, there's no freedom') were neatly demolished. He suggested I visit a couple of theological colleges in England and think and pray seriously about it.

That evening I was preaching at St Paul's, and a local headmaster came up to me afterwards and said, 'Stephen, I really think you ought to be in the ministry.' And several others that week said exactly the same, all independently. On the Friday, I knelt and said to the Lord, 'If that's where you want me, Lord, I'll go.' And he gave me a sense of peace as I resolved before him that I'd follow in that direction. Later, I found out that my parents had been praying that God would call me to full-time ministry – my mother's only disappointment was that she'd rather hoped it would be in the Methodist Church!

As anyone offering for the ordained ministry knows, it is one thing to know that God has called you; it's quite another getting the Church of England to recognise it!

Our full-time lay assistant at St Paul's, Geoff Powell, who'd been a teacher, suggested that I did an extra 'A' level in RE, as I had only one Physics with an 'E' grade pass. He suggested I take Religious Studies which concentrated on the scriptures and would serve as good background for my preaching. He tutored me over four months in my spare time. Job was the set Old Testament book. It truly came alive during my period of brokenness. When I began making enquiries about courses and grants, I discovered that having two 'A' levels would qualify me for a degree course and that the local Education authority would give me a grant. All this would save the Church of England three years of fees.

My summer holidays in England in 1979 included visits to two theological colleges and an interview with the Diocesan Director of Ordinands – whose churchmanship was poles apart from my own. He discovered as we talked that I'd not been confirmed, so suggested I should make immediate arrangements with the bishop. This was done, and was followed by a half-hour conversation in which the Bishop of Winchester agreed to sponsor me for an ACCM Selection Conference. It took place in Northampton in April 1980.

I was told two things before I went to the Selection Conference. First, relax and accept that God's will would be done. Second, don't try to preach at and convert the examiners or the other candidates. The day I left for England, my Bible reading included Revelation 3.8, 'Behold, I have set before you an open door, which no one is able to shut' . . . a promise which was later fulfilled.

ACCM conferences can be fun. There were about sixteen other candidates. Several were fellow evangelicals. We were set several exercises, performed in the presence of the examiners. One exercise was called a 'ten minute topic'. We were given a topic which we had to introduce (without notice or preparation) in two minutes, then lead a discussion for seven, then summarise in one minute. It gave the examiners the opportunity to see if we could be impartial in discussions, and if we were able to listen to other people's points of view. Each of us also had a thirty-minute interview with each of the five examiners. The Chairman wanted to know why I was at the ACCM conference. The Secretary wanted to know which college I preferred, and who would pay for the course (ACCM paid if you could not obtain an LEA grant).

This was my first experience of people from the high church wing of the Church of England. They seemed to genuflect at every opportunity!

Discussions with the examiners were interesting too –

topics included the authority of scripture, the Bible and science, and speaking in tongues.

The conference lasted three days. Just over a week later I heard I had been recommended for training. But then came a snag. The ACCM selectors had picked up that my experience had been mainly in evangelical circles. So the bishop's letter suggested that I chose carefully where I should train so that I would be exposed to the 'wider views of theological thinking'. The Diocesan Director of Ordinands wrote saying that this clearly ruled out any specifically evangelical colleges. He suggested another one which in my view was not right for me at all.

There was a series of polite letters between myself, the bishop and the DDO. Eventually the DDO backed down and I accepted the place I had been offered at St John's College, Nottingham for September 1980.

1980 to 1983 were difficult years. I had not expected some of the things that were presented to us. One or two staff had views of the scriptures which questioned their historical accuracy and truth. The problem was that none of us 'knew the rules'. It was like playing a theological game where those of us learning were not being told what the presuppositions were. I felt threatened because questions were being asked and assumptions made which cut across all I had previously assumed. I think I was one of only a minority who managed to maintain daily prayer and Bible reading – an indictment on the spirituality of theological training.

I was resident in the single students block on a corridor with eleven others. They included John from Nigeria, formerly an assistant principal at the pastors' college who had come to England for further study: he was a convert from Islam, and three other Steves – including one a very solid Yorkshireman whose rugby skills were matched by a deep love for Christ and for people.

My sense of humour infuriated some, and I like several others found myself becoming very defensive. I hid behind my identity as an 'overseas student from Jersey'. The training varied over the three years. Year one was a foundation year, with lectures in Old and New Testament background (there wasn't much study of what the Bible actually said!), church history, and spirituality. There was also a placement at a local church. I was sent to a congregation which had declined over recent years, and had combined with a neighbouring parish. The college had been asked to put a team of students in to help 'work it up'. Gradually, as the congregation increased, the team was reduced. We attended on Sundays, took part in services and did some visiting. Some of the team helped with a weeknight Pathfinder group. I did some visiting and occasionally preached.

Our second year was more academic. A lot of time was spent at the University of Nottingham. My car became known as the 'overseas students car' as I regularly chauffeured John from Nigeria, and Henry and Yeko from Uganda. They were all godly men and taught me a lot about humility, love and being positive about other people.

During that year we had sermon classes. A group of about ten, including a staff member, would go to a nearby church. One student would preach. His sermon, mannerisms, content, delivery and biblical accuracy would be dissected later by members of the group. Sometimes this could be destructive, especially if the student had little experience of preaching. But it was often helpful.

I remember once being due to preach at a church twenty miles from college. It was a morning communion, so we had to leave early. A number of things went wrong. When I entered the church with the vicar I knelt to pray at the prayer desk, not realising that what I thought was one large kneeler, was in fact three perched precariously. When weight was applied to the top one, the second moved away from the others, leaving me with my nose buried in the prayer desk.

When I got up to preach, I had competition in the form of a baby in the arms of its mother. It began to yell as soon as I began. I had to time my sentences for when the baby was drawing breath! I had not experienced such a problem before and in my naivety I struggled on while the vicar sat opposite, pretending he didn't hear or notice the commotion.

Finally, during the communion, I administered the cup, and ran out of wine. The vicar had to get more from the vestry, and forgot to pray over it – a point not unnoticed by the sermon class!

Another visit was to a church which had entered into renewal. A young man lead choruses on a guitar. At one point he made the congregation get up and jig around the church in procession to some inane chorus – at which point I and others wished we weren't there!

One Sunday the sermon class met a lady who had come to faith because of a dog! Her best friend used to attend worship and take her small dog to church. The lady died and her friend adopted the dog. When it heard the church bells it would make a beeline for the church. This kept happening for weeks until the lady's resistance ended and she began to come to church. She would take the dog to the rail when she went for communion. Whether the dog ever got a blessing from the clergy we never found out!

Our third year included further academic study, and a parish placement involving several sessions a week. We then had to write a 5,000 word placement report. This was very useful and I had some stretching times at what we would now call a UPA (Urban Priority Area) parish in Derby. I was faced with problems I had not personally encountered before – unemployment, broken homes, and broken people. My only involvement in a pantomime occurred there too – the church put on 'Snow White and the Seven Dwarfs'. I played Snow White's father. It brought more than 70 people together in the church and created fellowship and fun.

During that year the curacy hunt began in earnest. Winchester diocese had released me early to look at curacies in other dioceses. My college principal had thought (mistakenly) that I might want to return to the security of the Channel Islands. We had been told that the first curacy in particular was an extension of our college training and that finding the right vicar from whom we could learn was vital.

One or two places I looked at were clearly not right. In one the vicar's wife ran the parish. In another the parish staff were distinctly uncomfortable when I asked about conversions to Christ. 'That isn't the sort of language we use around here' was the retort. I was relieved that I was not offered the post!

In April 1983 I was put in contact with Colin Perkins, vicar of a group of country parishes in Nottingham. Initially he did not want someone straight from college because running six parishes needed a curate who could do communion services from the start. However, he agreed to see me and after a weekend trekking around the six parishes and eight churches, and having a week or so to think it over and pray, Colin offered me a post as curate.

That initial weekend was interesting. The soakaway at the vicarage got blocked. Colin found himself trying hard to keep the loos from blocking up while entertaining us. At one of the churches a prominent member of the congregation said to me 'Well if you're thinking of coming here as curate, ten minutes is quite long enough for a sermon!'

Ordination retreat came along, and we pranced around in cassocks for three days trying to be silent. (Have you ever asked someone to pass the salt at mealtimes without saying anything?) Then came the service itself. I can't remember much about it except that the preacher gave an excellent, encouraging address. Then it was off to start work.

At first I lived in the old vicarage in a village at the eastern end of the group of parishes. It had seen better days and was in urgent need of repairs. The three enormous bedrooms had no heating. There was just one electric socket per room and concrete floors, with correspondingly enormous supporting beams in the ceilings underneath. The bathroom had the largest bath I've ever seen – it must have been over seven feet long with choice chocolate-brown paintwork and enormous spiders. The servants' quarters along the back courtyard adjoining the property were delapidated but included a garage, stables for two horses, a hayloft and a wash-house, complete with an old 'copper' in the corner to boil clothes. The half-acre garden was overgrown as the previous curate had left some three months previously. The PCC had not done anything about it. This, I discovered, was typical of this particular village – plenty of talk but no decisions or action.

The diocese had been attempting to do something about the vicarage for years and before I moved in, when looking over the house with the Assistant Diocesan Secretary and Archdeacon we talked about the possibilities, as there were several modern houses for sale in the village. Eventually, some weeks after I'd been ordained, the diocese said they were selling the vicarage by auction and were going to buy one of the modern houses which were for sale. Then began the usual village problems: 'But it's *always* been the vicarage' 'It may be too large for a single man, they should have got a married one' and 'It doesn't matter what condition it's in, it *is* the vicarage'. I kept out of the arguments. The Archdeacon spoke at a special meeting of the PCC and eventually it agreed to the sale, although not without some dissension!

Colin, my vicar, and I met three times a week. On Mondays we met for prayer and a staff meeting, we would pray together each Saturday. Then on Wednesdays we met for Bible study, either at his vicarage or at mine. During staff meetings we worked through practical issues and pastoral problems. There were questions like how to lead the different services – we had a mixture of ASB, 1662 and family services, and these sometimes varied from parish to parish. Country parishes move very slowly, and although we used ASB Rite A for communion some of the time, primarily we used 1662. My experience of taking part in 1662 services was rather limited. My home church in Jersey had a rather 'free' style, and St John's College was not renowned for its use of the Book of Common Prayer! (To be fair, we used 1662 during Lent in two of my three years there.)

Mistakes did occur in services nevertheless. During one service of Morning Prayer at our tiniest parish of 68 inhabitants, of whom regularly ten to fifteen were in church (and many more at festivals), I opened my prayer book at Evening Prayer, which is identical for the first part of the service.

When I announced the Magnificat, the organist leaned over and whispered loudly, 'It's the *Psalm* next!'

At another church the organist had a bleeper on his key ring. If he mislaid the bunch a brief whistle would trigger a bleep to guide you to it. In one memorable service, as we sang the first hymn, he hit a certain note, and set the bleeper off. In the same church, some months after Julia and I were married, she was preaching after I had led the service. A sparrow had got into the building, and while she preached, it swooped from one side of the church to the other. When you're preaching there's nothing worse than that to distract you.

At the same church we often had a peacock perched on one of the gravestones outside the window, squawking from time to time. To keep the grass down the local farmer grazed his sheep in the churchyard. So there were occasions when members of the flock were outnumbered by real sheep – who would often come in the porch to listen!

Heating country churches is always a problem. Most were not built with warmth in mind. One parish church had its heating system out of order for quite some time during one cold spell. One Sunday the hymn 'Rescue the perishing' took on new meaning . . .

It was only after being out in the parish for a while that one could reflect on the training received at college and see how it fitted into parish ministry. College training was primarily academic theology – intellectual study of past and present theologians. It was weak on reading what the scripture actually said and applying it. Our preparation for ministry seemed to be more a matter of getting us through a course of study rather than leading us to be people of prayer. To maintain a personal walk with the Lord in daily prayer and Bible reading was not easy. We did have a course on 'spirituality' but courses are no good without people living lives of prayer and holiness. St John's did at least get us out into practical assignments in parishes and hospitals or factories where we worked alongside people in their place of work.

How, though, did it work out in the parish? I had been stretched intellectually, and that was important. But it is when you are engaged in real ministry – to the sick and dying, to the broken people, to the relatives of suicide victims – that you find that intellectual resources are no substitute for hearts of compassion, for love and for the Holy Spirit at work in us through prayer. The intellectual study on the other hand did – and does – help in understanding the cross and resurrection practically. An inadequate grasp of the cross and sufferings of Christ will lead to an inability to minister to those who suffer, physically or emotionally.

My relationship with Colin was important in helping me not only to work together with him for the Kingdom but also to develop my gifts, and recognise my weaknesses. Colin is a quick thinker. He could summarise theological issues rapidly and succinctly. Some of his sermons were super and some parishioners used to say they wished he'd speak more slowly, or repeat the sermons, because there were so many gems of teaching in them. On reflection I was headstrong and probably hard to teach. When you come out of college it is often with drive and enthusiasm which needs tempering with wisdom and realism. I was all for visiting as many people as I could to stir up interest in the Christian faith, to preach evangelistically and to see people come to Christ. Rita, Colin's wife, wisely said 'In the countryside, if you can move the churches on an inch or two, you've achieved a lot.'

Supervision was at a minimum on Sundays. With six parishes, each with its own weekly service, and two other chapels-of-ease (one shared with the Methodists) requiring one service every other week, Colin and I took services together maybe once a fortnight. That was a disadvantage in that Colin felt he couldn't give me enough training. It was an advantage in that I developed my own style and approach to worship and sermons. I was criticised by some because I constantly spoke evangelistically to established church members, who resented my questioning their spirituality. They may have been right, and I needed to learn to encourage and nurture them rather than confront. At the same time they needed to be woken out of the complacency of relying on the faith of the clergy rather than having their own personal faith in Christ. We did begin doing sermon series around the churches. This meant being able to preach the same sermons in different churches. We often did this with the monthly family services. Some families who 'followed' the family services around the group – each parish had it on a different Sunday – heard the same address more than once. One family got the same talk on prayer by me three weeks in a row. I did ask them whether they thought God was speaking to them about something! As Colin said, with so many churches, it meant we were never unpopular in all of them at the same time!

Colin and I did find it difficult at times – as in every relationship. We didn't differ on basic beliefs, but we often did things in different ways. One parishioner said to me, 'You can't put an old head on young shoulders.' I needed wisdom to temper the enthusiasm.

In the countryside communities are 'settled'. Most residents have lived there most of their lives and their families before them for generations. They'd seen vicars and curates come and go. There's a story about a churchwarden who always complained about the vicar until the vicar announced his resignation. Then he would be full of kind words so one vicar asked why he'd had a change of heart. The warden would reply, 'I've seen six vicars come and go, and every one of them has been worse than the previous one!'

There is much residual faith in such communities – often third or fourth hand. Nevertheless it is there. Often the experience of Christ and of worship has been restricted almost completely to what has happened on a Sunday in the local church. The assumption is that everyone is Christian anyway and that the vicar and curate are the ones who maintain a relationship with God on their behalf – why then should *they* read their Bibles and pray? One lady was shocked when I suggested in a sermon that we should pray for those outside the church. She said, 'Why should we pray for them?

They ought to do it themselves!' Getting people away from relying on *our* walk with the Lord was a difficult task.

People outside the church, though, would often show a real hunger for spiritual faith – a hunger which would not be nurtured in the worship of the local church. I visited quite a number of such people. One man recounted to me that he often watched people who went to church on a Sunday going past his house. He wondered why they went as the impression they created was that they didn't enjoy it anyway and came out with faces as long as those they had going in.

On a subsequent visit he told me that one of his bedrooms had an odd atmosphere and that he'd been told by the previous occupant that there was a ghost there. The room was always cold and sometimes strange smells were discernible. I asked him whether he wanted me to do something about it. He said, 'Yes, go up and see for yourself.' I did, the room was certainly strangely cold. I began to pray and it was as if something came at me, bounced off me and left. I asked the Lord to fill the place with his presence, and then retired downstairs. I told him if he had any more problems, to call me. A few weeks later I saw him again and he said, 'I don't know what you did, but the whole atmosphere of the cottage has changed. That room is warm and welcoming – I've been telling all my friends in the pub about it.' He later made a commitment to Christ and was eagerly reading the scriptures. He was never incorporated into the local church because it would have stifled his growth.

There was always suspicion of anyone new coming to church. In some parishes they were either viewed with hostility (one regular actually said to another villager who came to church unexpectedly 'What are *you* doing here?') or were ignored as if they weren't there. And if a comparative newcomer wanted to get involved in doing something in the church, the hostility grew!

During our third year in the parish my wife Julia and I went to Sheffield to hear John Wimber, an American pastor who has entered into healing ministry and evangelism in a big

way. We had heard of him, thanks to controversial comments reported concerning the late David Watson. Julia and
I wanted to hear first-hand what John Wimber had to say, so
that we could judge for ourselves. (Our daughter Joanna,
then eleven weeks old, went with us in a carry-cot!)

The four days of meetings, in our view, were largely
uncontroversial. John Wimber was saying things about the
healing ministry of Jesus, the place of 'signs and wonders'
and other manifestations within the evangelistic ministry of
the church, which we had always wanted to believe, but were
afraid actually to voice. This is not to say we accepted
everything we heard and saw but we experienced real Spirit-
led worship, with no attempt to whip up an atmosphere.
After half an hour of worship John Wimber or one of his
associates gave a lecture on aspects of the healing ministry of
Jesus, illustrating it with their own successes and failures in
praying for the sick. After a coffee break, John Wimber held
what he called a 'clinic', in that he asked us to stand and to
wait for the Holy Spirit to move in power among us. He
simply prayed, 'Come, Holy Spirit', and within a few
moments people in the auditorium became affected – some
seemed to be 'lost in wonder, love and praise' as they quietly
worshipped the Lord. Others quietly wept. A tiny handful
(out of a couple of thousand) began to moan or scream. John
Wimber pointed out that this was probably an emotional
release. Many British people have very suppressed
emotions.

Julia and I observed and listened over the four days, but
we kept out of praying for others even though we were
encouraged to do so. We returned home, knowing that the
Lord had been there but not being quite sure of all we had
heard and seen. I was unhappy about the approach in the
seminars on ministering to and praying for the physically ill.
The seminar seemed to concentrate entirely on waiting on
the Lord till he seemed to give a word of knowledge or a
picture about someone present who was ill. For example
someone seemed to visualise an elbow – was there anyone
there who had an elbow problem? If there was they would

pray for healing. But I wanted to know about how to pray effectively for those I already knew who were ill.

John Wimber said at the end of the conference, 'Some of you will be wondering, what will we do when we get home to our churches? Don't do anything for the moment. Do nothing, let it all simmer and let God lead you.' He echoed our private thoughts and on our return we said very little about what we'd seen. One week after the conference I had the worst bout of asthma for over twenty years, something I'd grown out of at eleven or twelve!

But in the ensuing weeks and months, things began to happen. A couple who had little contact with the church (the husband wanted nothing to do with the church and the Christian faith) had serious difficulties. He lost his job and I called to talk with him. He 'backed off' but on Christmas Eve he and his wife came to the midnight communion service. As they came to the rail for a blessing (neither was confirmed) the Lord met with them. On my return from our after-Christmas break I discovered they had both come to Christ. Julia and I took them and another couple through a nine-week course on the basics of the Christian faith and they are now both active members of their local church.

On another occasion a lady who had severe psoriasis on her knees (a skin condition) came to our quarterly healing service. Within days it had almost completely healed. We began to see the power of God work through us.

What the Lord did at that conference was to give us a new confidence to pray for the sick, as well as a new power to sometimes see him heal. Neither of us had any overwhelming experiences but we did have a new sense of the Lord at work in us and through us. And that work has carried on since.

With thanks to Mrs Ann Hailes who kindly typed the manuscript from my handwritten notes; and to Colin and Rita Perkins whose patience and ministry taught me much.

Stephen Mourant is now vicar of Old Harlow, Essex.

Chapter Six

FILLING THE BREACH

by

Kathryn Pritchard

I was a pale young curate then

W. S. Gilbert

Why did I go into the ministry? One thing stands out in my mind as I look back: I never once had a clear call to be ordained, there was no 'writing-on-the-wall' experience.

I studied Modern Languages at university and, like many of my contemporaries, was very unclear as to my future career as the final year approached. During the previous year I had worked as an English Assistant in Lille, Northern France. It was a very eventful year. I spent my weekends with a dynamic, young Christian community. Many of their weekends were spent in street evangelism in the pedestrian precincts of Lille, they were also developing a ministry of hospitality to the homeless. While there I also mixed with youths involved with Christian missionary organisations whose concern was to reach young people in urban Europe. I returned to England to complete my college course, hoping to return to France or Belgium in some capacity.

However, the next step was a year's postgraduate diploma in interpreting and translating at Bradford University. Familiar story: at the end of this year I was stumped for my next move. Language jobs were scarce, none of my foreign options seemed feasible and I couldn't quite muster the enthusiasm to fill in entry forms for the Civil Service (my last resort!).

I haven't yet mentioned that during this time my mother had been completing a part-time course to train as a deaconess. This was one option that had never occurred to me: I had mixed feelings about women in formal church leadership (I didn't know any!) and had no desire to be involved with what I perceived as clerical irrelevance – robes, bazaars and churchy respectability. Mum, undeterred, suggested I might make a good deaconess – my response was to laugh at the suggestion, I couldn't see myself in that role at all!

That was in September 1983. In February 1984 I learned of a mission which was the brainchild of Brandon Jackson, provost of Bradford Cathedral and a team of local church leaders and business people. Local business people were to be invited to continental breakfasts in the delightful surroundings of one of Bradford's poshest hotels. While there they would hear David MacInnes speaking about the relevance of the Gospel for their lives. I jumped at the chance to be involved in such an imaginative project.

A couple of weeks later I went to the cathedral to spend part of the day packaging the books and leaflets that our guests were to receive along with their croissants and coffee. Once ensconced in my little downstairs room, feeling rather grand to be working at the cathedral, I realised that I had forgotten to bring any sellotape. I went upstairs to the main cathedral office in search of sellotape and bumped into a clergyman who was introduced as the precentor. 'Excuse my ignorance but what does a precentor do?' I asked. He explained and added meaningfully: 'I also look after candidates for the ministry.'

'Oh,' I said.

'Are you interested?' he asked.

'Well . . . vaguely.'

He asked a few more questions and invited me to come and see him the following week.

When we saw each other next, we had a long chat about me – my hopes, fears and dreams. It was a surprise to me when at the end of our time together he asked me if I would consider going to a Selection Conference for the Anglican ministry. I don't know whether it was fatigue, uncertainty about the future, or the gentle prod of God's Spirit, but I was less averse to the idea than I had been six months previously. Besides, I had recently come into contact with people of my own age who were off to train for the ministry – one friend was even going to the college where it was suggested I train – that made me feel better about the whole prospect.

My ACCM took place that September and two weeks later I was on my way to Cranmer Hall, St John's College, Durham – quite the permanent student it would appear! I must have gone to Durham with a rather idealistic picture of life at theological college – because it wasn't what I expected it to be.

I made some good friends and we had great times together, although I was surprised and initially a little disappointed that we were such an ordinary bunch of people. There were lectures, seminars and special courses to attend along with church placements, but the focus was very much on what was happening inside me. I had my fears and insecurities as a person, my image of God was badly in need of repair, and I needed to work through the way I related with those around me at the college. I also struggled through endless doubts as to my suitability for clerical ministry: 'I'm too young to become an institution!' was my heartfelt cry. Would people still treat me normally after ordination or would I end up in splendid isolation in a parish somewhere? How could you be truly feminine in clerical gear? Would life ever be fun again after college? Was God even concerned?

I did not go through that process alone. Many of my close friends at Durham had similar ups and downs, even considering whether or not to leave – had it all been a mistake? Somebody told me later that often when we are right in the centre of God's purposes for us, we have little or no sense of assurance of this being so. The reassurance only comes as we persevere on through our doubts and on to our destination. That, I believe, is a very apt observation on the experience of training for the ministry and afterwards.

My time at Durham did me good. I emerged from the process considerably mellowed and matured with, I suspect, greater reality and substance to my faith in God. It had also begun to dawn on me by the end of my training that God was calling Kathryn Pritchard – not some stereotypical woman minister – to offer herself for ministry, and that he was wanting to draw the best out of me, not squash me into a mould.

My years at Cranmer also firmly established me in the belief that having fun, good friends and creative outlets (in my case singing lessons and the occasional dance class) are vital to balance the serious issues you face in life and ministry. Life shouldn't just revolve around church work – there needs to be balance otherwise your ministry gets out of perspective. I remain committed to that view!

In September 1987 I moved down to London to begin work as a curate in a busy Croydon parish.

I was quite fearful of the move and of the whole process of uprooting and re-adjusting. It took me a good part of that first year to adjust to the demands of a new job, a new crowd of people and a new area.

The worst thing was the initial loneliness. I found it a rude shock to be living on my own for the first time, planted in a large three-bedroomed terraced house, bereft of soul mates, college friends and family. In my initial pessimism I found it hard to believe that things would get better! For the first three months I felt very low.

It didn't seem to help that I was in a parish where people welcomed me warmly. I didn't feel free to go round responding to peoples' polite concern with 'Actually, I'm feeling miserable.' I had arrived in the church as a 'professional' minister and couldn't just go splurging out my feelings without testing the ground first. It takes time in any situation to establish trust between people, especially when you are working out that delicate balance between openness and discretion in a new role. Consequently, I worked hard arranging to go out and meet up with friends on my day off. Some weeks I was too tired or depressed to go trekking across London. Phone calls home and to old friends were very frequent.

Of course, it's just when you're feeling a mere shadow of

your former self that you need to be at your most sociable and lively. There are so many people to meet and names to remember and it all takes energy which you don't feel you possess – you are only operating on one cylinder when you need to be at full strength.

The friendship situation began to improve four or five months after my arrival in Croydon. I started to gel with a few people in the parish and then I got a housemate (a real answer to a somewhat lame prayer!) which made a tremendous difference to my sense of well-being. It was great to come home at night and discuss or moan about what had gone on that day. She attended another local church, which made it easier for me to talk about work without putting either of us in an awkward position. Things started to feel good socially – I felt that I had found my feet.

The working relationship with the vicar – the training incumbent – is crucial for the new curate's well-being and however hard you try there are bound to be ups and downs. Your vicar, with all his years of experience, is still mortal and won't always relate to you perfectly. You might find that he doesn't like delegating and you end up with too little to do Alternatively, he may have been waiting eagerly for your arrival to off-load all the tedious tasks onto you. Like all relationships it can be a changeable one: your vicar may be alternately employer; friend; enthusiastic fellow searcher after truth; squasher of bright ideas; happy; anxious and so on.

Even if you have found the perfect trainer, he won't always operate as you do. Learning to communicate and understand each other's working patterns and expectations is vital. I say all this with great assurance *now* – but I know I didn't really understand what made me tick as a work colleague when I first arrived in the parish, let alone being able to communicate that to my vicar. We learned to relate as colleagues in a rather hit-and-miss way. We were both eager to make it work and were both up front, fairly choleric characters and this led to some tense as well as fruitful exchanges. However, there is no painless or risk-free method of learning to communicate honestly. I would encourage people to look for training incumbents who are open to working at this side of things – it makes all the difference to how you feel about your curacy. Sometimes it can feel like an arranged marriage without any of the fun!

Workwise I found the first few months hectic and exhausting. I observed my vicar in various 'bread-and-butter' activities: funerals and funeral visits, home communions, marriage rehearsals, baptism preparation and so on. I also attended anything and everything that went on in church. The work delegated to me was gradually increased: I took funerals; carried out routine administrative tasks; preached; led Sunday worship; chose hymns and music for services.

In the early stages I can't say that anything I was doing afforded me great satisfaction – it was all too new and strange. I felt oddly detached from what I was doing. Leading Sunday worship, for instance, seemed very impersonal.

Highlights were a couple of funerals where the families really seemed to take me to their hearts. At least temporarily I felt I was doing something meaningful. Were people actually drawn closer to God as a result of my ministry – or was that a naive dream of bygone days? Sometimes I did feel like a dusty old cleric, institutionalised before my time.

Generally, everything started to come together half-way into my first year. Life was fine at home, friendships blossomed and this dovetailed with feeling at home in the job and more able to be myself. God had seemed rather distant during the early time of adjustment but I started to regain a sense of his reality and warmth.

Like most of us I function best when I am known and loved, warts and all, and as I sensed this happening my work became far more rewarding. As spring approached there was a new lightness in my step. I seemed to have more of a knack with things I had previously agonised over, such as sermon preparation. I became enthusiastic about issues such as the pastoral opportunities thrown up by baptism and began to look at ways of making the preparations more effective.

There were opportunities to be creative with words and music in informal services. I was also involved in the planning and leading of a stimulating Christian lifestyle course. All these chances to be creative and take initiatives were important for my sense of fulfilment – but it had taken time for them to emerge.

It was also at this stage, around March, that I learned of my vicar's unexpected appointment to a senior church post – he was to leave in September, just one year after my arrival. This, as you can imagine, did wonders for concentrating the mind on the job in hand – after I had got over the shock!

Of course it did take a while to get over the shock and the initial sense of let-down. It was tempting to feel like a tragic heroine – so much for being eased into the job gradually! Then, friends started to make encouraging noises about all the opportunities for growth and ministry that an inter-regnum would present, so I began to view it as a challenge, not as the end of the world. In the end I was fortunate that our 'vicarless' period only lasted until mid-January and I was able to gain a lot from the experience.

There is nothing like increased responsibility for galvanising all sorts of undeveloped talents. I was obliged to become more organised, have clear work priorities and not take on more than I could realistically cope with. I found my thinking becoming far more business-like and I became clearer and more assertive in the way I communicated with others. I had previously erred on the apologetic side when I asked people to do things – after all, who was I to tell people what to do?

Being a trainee curate is, initially at least, quite a low key role – you've always got the vicar to bail you out! Now, in a new situation, I felt the need to be more assured particularly in the public aspects of the job. As I projected greater confidence I actually felt more confident in most areas of ministry, especially leading services and preaching. I also sensed that I was starting to develop my own personal style rather than feeling like a pale imitation of my training vicar.

I don't want to give the impression that I was, at any stage, a one-woman-band. Ours is a church where lay leadership is developed in most areas. Moreover, I had the help and support of a part-time, non-stipendiary minister for the whole of the interregnum – he helped especially with preaching and leading of worship. As far as the day to day running of the parish was concerned the responsibility was mine, but here again I worked closely with our church secretary, whose efficiency was crucial for the smooth running of the interregnum. Nevertheless, for the whole of the time we were 'vicarless', I had a fresh view of everything I did, very much enjoying the scope I had been given. It was up to me, for instance, to choose and order study material for confirmation, baptism and centralised study groups, to plan the shape of the Christmas services and activities, to co-ordinate those involved in different areas of ministry, and generally to have my finger on the pulse – which I enjoyed.

Of course, all this responsibility made for increased stress – sometimes I longed for things to be back to normal – but knowing I could survive an interregnum increased my confidence no end and helped me think more positively about future possibilities for ministry.

Here are some practical tips for anyone finding themselves in that position:

1) Get an answerphone, it will keep you sane and enable you to take time off to watch favourite tv programmes undisturbed.

2) Employing someone to come in and do the cleaning every couple of weeks is a great boon if you have no-one to share the tasks with – and even if you have!

3) Have clear priorities for your time in charge and don't expect to achieve too much, your task is really to keep the show on the road.

4) Discover exactly who does what and carefully delegate activities and tasks that you don't have to handle personally – I even did this for funerals, asking local part-time clergy to cover those during the interregnum.

5) Don't forget that when a church is without an

incumbent it is the church wardens, technically, who have overall charge – if you work well with them they can back you up if things go badly wrong.

Of course, one thing about being a woman in ministry in the Church of England is that for practical purposes your licence to minister is a bit like a provisional driving licence – you always need someone else in the car with you! At first this didn't bother me. After all, I was very new to the experience of church ministry. However, particularly when all my male contemporaries were priested, it did begin to grate that just because I'm a woman I needed to have another minister ferried in for services of Holy Communion – it sometimes felt like a liturgical put down, communicating to others that in the eyes of the church a woman is not a complete minister. I know too, just how much I gained from the support of my male colleague but occasionally it made me fume when people assumed that because he took the priestly role on Sunday, he was in charge and carrying the bulk of the work on his shoulders. I found myself getting very sensitive about this – indeed I was surprised at how hurt I sometimes felt.

During this period I also detected within myself the seeds of workaholism – something I had wondered at in so many Christian ministers. It was so easy to end up functioning on an 'adrenalin-high', particularly during the very pressured build-up to Christmas. It was quite hard to come back down to earth in January when our new minister arrived: I found myself trying to regain that busy feeling rather than taking time to relax, have fun and wind down.

Since the arrival of my new training incumbent in January, we've made a fairly smooth transition into a new phase in our church life.

Yes, it does take time to get off one's temporary high horse and knuckle down to ordinary, crisis-free curatehood. I feel, however, that I've moved on to a new, more mellow phase in my training and the stability of the situation is doing me good. Some of my new-found efficiency disappeared with the advent of our new vicar but at least I know that it's down there somewhere waiting to be re-ignited! Anyway, I hope this highly personal view will provide pointers for those considering or training for ordained ministry.

Kathryn Pritchard is parish deacon at St Mary's Addiscombe, Croydon.

Chapter Seven

CITY CENTRE MINISTRY

by

Stephen Wookey

My dear child, you must believe in God in spite of what the clergy tell you

Benjamin Jowett

Some years ago I met up with an old school friend I had not seen for years. 'I'm not surprised,' he said on learning that I was going to be ordained, 'you always were the religious sort.' To this day I am not sure why the remark so annoyed me. Perhaps it was because when I thought of my time at school, and all that had happened since, I wished he would recognise how much I'd changed. I had not thought about ordination then, nor did my family expect it, although my grandfather had been ordained late in life.

It was only when I went up to university that I began to understand what Christ had done for me, and became committed to him. Everything was new, and my whole perspective changed. Even sport, which till then had dominated my thinking and my time, faded in importance. I still loved playing football, and particularly cricket, but sport had ceased to be the main attraction. I wanted others to know of Christ, and I began to consider some kind of full-time service.

It does seem strange to look back at my call. It is hard to discern between one's own desires, a sense of obligation and the genuine voice of God. How easy to have a rather starry-eyed vision of the ministry as one long mission, endless conversions, powerful sermons: after all, is not that what the hagiographies all tell us? It is quite a shock to face the reality of parish life, to witness the sinfulness of even the greatest of saints, to see the tragedy of Christian marriage break-up, and to realise that no family is free from its share of skeletons in the cupboard. But the things that attracted me to the ministry have not dimmed with time and if anything have become more sharply focussed: the wonder of the gospel, its absolute relevance to every age, and the joy of seeing changed lives. If the gospel is truly good news for all, what greater privilege could there be than to spend one's whole life proclaiming that good news?

Nevertheless, I wrestled for some time with the thought of the ministry. In the initial enthusiasm of my conversion I longed for some way to give expression to the new life and purpose that I had found. Since I had been brought up an Anglican, and most of those people that I knew who were involved in full-time Christian service were Anglican ministers, the Anglican route seemed the most logical. To say that I had studied the thirty-nine Articles and found that they most accurately represented my theological stance would be less than the truth – indeed it is only over the last few days that I have come to understand the depth and theology of the Prayer Book, and recognise the relative poverty of the ASB. How far, then, can a new believer's enthusiasm together with encouragement from friends constitute a true call? Certain passages from the scriptures influenced my thinking, but it was a combination of advice and my own inclination that tipped the balance. But as I look back I become more than ever convinced of, and grateful for, the sovereignty of God. For there was a stage when I became terrified that I had missed God's plan for my life, that whatever I attempted for him next would be only second-best. In my pride, I believe, I had decided what I would do, and never stopped to ask if this really was the Lord's will. As I look back now I see things differently. Did not my Lord know what I would do? Did he not see the choices I would make in advance? Did he not have the power still to work in me 'according to his good pleasure' (Eph 1.9)? Had God somehow ceased to be God, just because my motives were mixed?

When I finally came to a decision I was doing a fill-in year after university. The usual round of interviews and the inevitable ACCM conference followed, and I headed off to theological college for my training. People tend to deride their training as being the last thing to equip them for the ministry itself. But I have to admit that I rather enjoyed my time at theological college. Perhaps I did not apply myself enough to discover its weaknesses – it is one of my regrets that I wasted too much time at college – but I still feel it is too easy to criticise. The chance to study the Bible in depth, to wrestle with the great doctrines, to think through so many complex ethical issues, and to face the challenge of different Christian traditions was one that I will always be grateful for. But perhaps my understanding of the nature of the minister's task is somewhat different today. Preaching and teaching have taken up a great deal of my time since those days at college, and there the training was a little deficient. A few lectures, a few trial sermons, and another inexperienced and rather gauche preacher was let loose on the church. In fact, the training I did receive came largely from house-parties that I used to attend.

I could also have done with more challenge to my devotional life. It seemed to be assumed that we were praying and studying the Bible when for many of us the actual daily devotions or quiet times had begun to dry up. It is hard to keep up one's devotional reading of the Word at 7.30, when at 10.00 one would have to dissect that same Word for the purposes of an essay. Such comments are truisms for all involved in theological education.

What I most regret as I look back is the lack of any general sense of the purpose of our education. There was and is a world to win, and our training made sense only if it would equip us better for that task. And yet, the vision of men and women lost without Christ, and in desperate need of the traditional evangelical gospel was somehow obscured. How challenged I was one day to be told by Bishop Stephen Neill, whom I feared, but respected for his courage, insight, and willingness even to rebuke when necessary, that we did not seem to pray for non-believers as theological students in his day prayed. How sad I feel too that the apostolic emphasis on the priority of the gospel – as the only hope for sinful man and woman – was so quickly submerged by the call to ecumenism, the insights of modern psychology and on occasion a patronisingly superior attitude to those who still believed in the old, old story.

In fact, the danger of distraction is no less real in the ministry itself. I have constantly to relearn the lesson that it is only the gospel that gives meaning to the work we do and must have the highest priority. How many of us have all but given up in prayer, and have allowed our ministries to be swallowed up by church politics, pastoral crises and sheer drudgery?

Nevertheless, I am grateful for the emphasis on study, and the way one's half-baked ideas on the atonement, or the Trinity were shown up for what they were, for the daily discipline of morning chapel (although a friend of mine once called it the last thing he did before he woke up!), and for the unfailing good humour and diligence of the staff. After all theological students must be among the most arrogant and critical of all audiences.

It was whilst I was at college that I became aware of what I call the 'if only' syndrome that has marked much of my thinking. At university I had not found personal devotional discipline particularly easy, but I used to put it down to the lack of routine that is a feature of student life. If only I could get into a job, and a regular routine, then personal Bible study and prayer would be so much easier. When I did move into a job I often found myself too tired to spend much time with God, and longed for the time to give myself unhurriedly to him. Theological college seemed the obvious answer. I arrived at college, but found that academic study, without the chance to put into practice what I was learning, made my quiet times rather dull and dry. I needed to be in a parish. It was only when I arrived in a parish that I found the excuses had dried up. Bible study and prayer would always be a battle, and if I could not win it in one situation I was unlikely to win it in another.

After three years at theological college I arrived in my first
parish, Christ Church Cockfosters. It was a church that I
knew by repute, and would probably be many people's
conception of the typical suburban evangelical congregation. I spent four happy years there and look back on the
church with much affection and gratitude. I found my
personal and working relationship with my vicar to be
remarkably free from difficulty – I have found that to be true
in all three churches where I have worked, although perhaps
my vicars would not agree! – and I owe him a great deal. It
was at Cockfosters that I learnt so many of the nuts and bolts
of ministry. However often one listens to lectures on pastoral
problems, nothing can quite prepare one for the first time –
the trauma of losing a 16-year-old girl from cancer, the cot
death of a 3-month-old boy born to parents who had almost
given up hope of having children, or the shock of the suicide
of a much-loved son, and the inevitable feelings of guilt and
recrimination afterwards. I also learnt how to take a wedding without dropping the ring down the grate, and to take
baptisms without dropping the baby (though not without
making them cry!).

My main area of responsibility at Cockfosters was the
youth work. There are many things that I wish I had done
differently, and that I had to learn the hard way, but it was
work that I enjoyed immensely. I will always remember one
particular houseparty where we were conscious of God's
working in a new way, and realised that it was 'not by might,
nor by power, but by my Spirit' (Zec 4.3). But I also came to
learn that we should never be fooled by numbers. Youth
group numbers fluctuate, at times quite violently, and therefore it is wise to concentrate on a few. Those few people
worked with and built up will reap a better harvest than
many who prove to be simply spectators.

Cockfosters was great fun. We always seemed to be laughing at staff meetings. Partly this was because of the endless
fund of stories that Don (my vicar) possessed: of how he
once served up bread and butter for a communion service
by mistake, of how his dog had once ruined an open air sale

by howling all the way through, and so on. But it was also because Don himself found names very difficult to remember. And it was nothing personal, since he would frequently forget the names of his curates as well. Needless to say, we played mercilessly on this. I have fond memories of staff meetings when we were discussing the format of the following Sunday's services, and he would happily arrange for Keith to lead the service (Keith being a former curate who had left three years ago) and for Andrew to take the prayers, despite the fact that Andrew was now running the daughter church up the road!

Indeed it has been a privilege to work for all four of the vicars I have served under. They have been understanding, long-suffering and have had great senses of humour. I only wish that I had told them how much they had given me. A hospital visit I completely messed up – I will always remember how Don took me aside and gently explained how I might do it another time. Times when I was no doubt the cause of complaints to the vicar and he took all the blame. All those days I have taken off to play cricket, or golf – for the honour of the diocese of course – and never made to feel guilty.

After four years I moved out to France to work at St Michael's, the English-speaking church in the centre of Paris. I spoke almost no French when I arrived, and not much more when I left, but it was wonderful to have been there. There were many similarities in the work – after all people have the same needs the world over and the gospel remains the same – but I came to realise the peculiar opportunities and strategic importance of city-centre ministry. There is much loneliness in the heart of the big cities, often leading to a much greater openness to the gospel. When people are removed from all that gives them their security – their homes, their friends, even their own language – it often raises questions that they might never otherwise ask. People used to turn up at services, never before having been to a church, or not for years, simply because we spoke English, or because we offered friendship in a hostile

world. And sometimes they would respond to the
gospel.

One Ash Wednesday, although the church was closed, I
was preparing for the evening service. The doorbell went,
and I answered it reluctantly since I had other things on my
mind and I had horrible visions of yet another person hoping
to get money. A young man was standing there. He had that
week committed himself to Christ and could I help him? It
was wonderful to see the way in which God dealt with him
over the following weeks.

There were many such stories. There was the Swedish
shipping insurance broker, recently arrived in Paris, who
spotted the English church on a map and thought he would
turn up. It had been at least eight years since he had been to a
church and Christian things were very far from his mind, but
he simply had nothing to do. He is, as I write, about to begin
at missionary training college. Then there was the dancer
recently arrived from Sun City where, amazingly, he had
been converted. He gave his testimony at a midweek meeting. 'I'm sorry this is taking so long to tell you,' he remarked
in his best Margate accent, 'but I'm trying desperately hard
not to swear.'

Each week seemed to bring its own extraordinary collec-
tion of stories. 'Can I help you?' I asked a gentleman
surveying our notice board one day. 'Oh yes,' he replied, 'I
want a wife.' He then assured me that he would prove to be
an excellent catch. I recall murmuring something about that
not being the sort of service we offered, and suggested he look
in the personal columns of a newspaper! One moment I was
trying to talk a young lad out of joining the Foreign Legion,
another trying to help someone escape from it. Then there
was the endless succession of people who had lost their
money or their passports and wanted us to get them home.
Sometimes such interruptions caused a real sense of frustration – surely I was not ordained for this! – but at others
they gave wonderful opportunities for the gospel.

I learnt in Paris a little more about the sort of community
that a church can be. In North London people had belonged

not just to their church, but also to their families who may or may not have been church members, and to friends they had grown up with. In Paris the church had to provide the home that people no longer had. We were quickly thrown close together. Often it made parting all the harder, and people were continually leaving Paris for all corners of the globe, but it did mean we shared more than we might have done in our own countries. I will never forget some of the services there: the feeling of intimacy, of home, of the presence of God. The reality of one's faith can be all the more vivid in a strange land.

I also learnt to be more of a realist. For nearly a year I was caught up in a rather disturbing episode involving anonymous letters and phonecalls. It became quite unpleasant, but at the same time perhaps it appealed to a certain sense of drama in me. We were in the front line, and this was a sign of that. We prayed, we fasted and we tried to talk it through with different people. We eventually discovered that we had been deceived all along by a church member. It was quite a humbling experience, but it taught me much. Spiritual things are not always all they seem, and it is easy to be taken in as a Christian because someone uses the right language. 'The people of this world are more shrewd in dealing with their own than are the people of the light' (Lk 16.8). There were other times when I was taken in and I became much more cynical about human nature. At least it was a salutary lesson.

There are not many places one can go to for a third curacy, and I had little idea what lay ahead after my time in Paris when the possibility arose of going to All Souls, Langham Place. For many years I had known and admired the church, but had never thought I might work there. Yet when the opportunity came I never doubted that it was the right time to move.

I have now been at All Souls for just over two years and find it endlessly fascinating and challenging. What is it like, I am sometimes asked, to work with Richard Bewes? To

preach before John Stott, when half your sermon is probably
filched from one of his commentaries anyway? How can you
get to know everyone? I used to think of All Souls, and other
large churches, as being full of extraordinary people. One
now realises that it is made up of a large number of ordinary
people. They have the same needs, the same pains and joys
as anyone else. They are not all super-saints, though there
are enough to keep one feeling pretty humble by comparison.

It is hard to foster a sense of unity of the whole body. In
Christ we are all one, and this church particularly illustrates
the wonder of this. To look out on the congregation, and to
see the huge number of different cultures represented, is to
have just a tiny glimpse of what it will be like among that
'great multitude which no man could number, from every
nation, from all tribes and peoples and tongues (Rev 7.9).
And yet one cannot know them all; and how can they be
enabled to be participants rather than spectators? This, and
the desire to unite many of different cultures and backgrounds in the work of the gospel, takes up much of my time.

I have become more than ever conscious of two areas that
should have concerned me before. First, only now have I
begun to grasp that it is the work of the gospel alone that
makes sense of the minister's calling. A minister's time can
easily be swallowed up in meetings, pastoral support or with
those facing some sort of crisis, and the daily grind of
administration. But though vital in church life these things
do not in themselves constitute our *raison d'être*. We are called
to go into all nations and preach the gospel, and in all that we
do we must never lose sight of that. Consequently I often
have to ask myself: is my apathy and tendency to get
sidetracked because I do not really believe in the gospel? The
danger of clerical professionalism rears its ugly head. I
preach, I teach, I encourage others because it is my job,
rather than because it is the most important task in the
world. How easy to lose the vision of a world without Christ!

My role at All Souls is as Director of Pastoring with
responsibility for the running of numerous fellowship
groups, and the support of the leaders. It is a huge task and

the second lesson that I am learning concerns strategy. With something over one hundred leaders to look after, in addition to the usual demands of ministry, I cannot do all that is needed. But to concentrate on some areas of ministry inevitably leads to other areas being neglected, and subsequent misunderstanding and resentment. Why does one have so much of the minister's time, when another has so little? Too much time has been spent running around plugging gaps or meeting demands, and too little planning about how to build for the future. But thinking is hard work: far easier just to keep the wheels in motion.

I find this is particularly true working in a famous church such as All Souls. The long distinguished traditions make one fearful to change anything – after all if All Souls has done it this way for so long it must be right. There are two traps. Either, anxious to make a mark, one rushes around making changes everywhere; or fear of changing anything means nothing moves on. I am slowly learning that I must never be afraid to make mistakes, and equally never afraid to admit them. Too often the fear of going wrong has prevented me from doing what I should. But too often also I have been too proud to admit mistakes.

I remember people advising me before I was ordained, and try to work out what I wish they had said. I was warned that loneliness would be a problem. In fact I have worked in three churches where it has not been hard to make friends, where people have been extremely kind and understanding, and I have not been lonely much. But I am aware nonetheless that there can be, as Amy Carmichael once put it, 'an awful loneliness in leadership'. I see it in some of my friends who work in quite different situations, and sometimes in myself.

There can be a particular pressure on those of us who are single. More and more people coming in to the ministry now are married, but for those of us who have stayed single – not in my case through any particular choice – it can be hard to come home to an empty pad late of an evening, to find the morning's breakfast things still unwashed, and this week's

layer of dust from the adjoining building site remaining to be
swept. But I find that I have freedom that many of my
married friends envy, I can spend much more of my time
with others in the church, and the older I get the more I fear
the thought of losing my independence. But it does lead to a
certain vulnerability. I read, with a real sense of dread, of
those clergy who have been found out in some form of sexual
misdemeanour, and realise how easily it could be me. 'Let
any one who thinks that he stands take heed lest he fall' (1
Cor 10.12).

I remember being told that the first thing to go in parish life,
apart from one's prayer life, would be one's reading. I
therefore started with great resolutions about taking time to
read and study. But how right they were. Reading can so
easily become simply reading for the next sermon or talk,
keeping one step ahead of the congregation – and not always
that! I am grateful for the stimulus at my present church of
knowing that the church will be full, and that tapes of the
sermon will go all over the world. I hate the apprehension
before, but it helps concentration. But how much study do I
do beyond that? Not much, in all honesty. Write a book, I
was once told, as a way of continuing to study. Does a
chapter in a book about curates qualify?
    When it comes to what I do read I seem to return more and
more to the old masters. Is it because I live in the past, or
simply that there is in the old classics, whether they be the
Puritans, the Wesleys, M'Cheynes, Baxters or Ryles, a
depth, a learning and a wealth of understanding and experience that we cannot touch today? Even Spurgeon's *Lectures to
my Students*, which incidentally I wish that I had read while at
college (as I do Baxter's *Reformed Pastor*), has a breath of
wisdom that amazes me. And I am often humbled by the
commitment they showed to the ministry.
    There are two things that I wish I had realised earlier. The
first is the importance of personal holiness. I often think of
the words of St Augustine, 'To my fellow man a heart of love.
To my God, a heart of flame. To myself, a heart of steel.'

There is surely no greater thing that we can give to those we serve than our own personal holiness. Perhaps too there is no area where I am more conscious of my own failure. We often smile a little knowingly at the rather quaint media image of the old, other-worldly vicar. But in our worldly wisdom many of us could do with a little of his personal sanctity. It strikes me that the man or woman of true holiness is universally recognised, and indeed admired, however much he or she is made fun of. We often object to the traditional caricature of the vicar, but it seems preferable to the more modern idea of the trendy, with-it cleric who will do anything to be one of the troops.

Robert Murray M'Cheyne wrote, 'What a man is alone on his knees before his God, that he is and nothing else.' Prayer never ceases to be a struggle, and yet is it not the most important factor in determining the worth of our ministry? Again, I seem to spend ages considering different ideas and techniques, all of which masquerade as being the key to success, while forgetting that nothing of lasting value will be achieved without prayer.

Second there is the importance of Christian friendship. It may seem odd that someone involved in ministry needs to learn about that, but it is all too easy for the minister to become isolated. The New Testament constantly enjoins us to encourage, build up, urge one another on and yet there is, in me, and in many of my friends a strange reticence to talk about those things very close to the heart. It might be typical English, middle class, public school reserve, but I tend to think that the older we get as Christians, and the more mature, the harder it becomes to ask each other awkward questions and to be honest about our own failings.

I am sad about those with whom I trained, whom I let down by not being a better friend. Perhaps I have not kept in touch with them, maybe not inquired after their walk with Christ. I think increasingly that the further one goes on in ministry, the more important it becomes to encourage one another.

I am often told that I guard my privacy very jealously and

I am beginning to realise what a danger that can be. Part of it is inevitable. As a curate I am a public person, and much of my life is open for public inspection. I therefore seek all the more avidly for times on my own, or when I can choose what I do. But when outside the public gaze, it can be tempting to live another life altogether. After all if no one can see, what does it matter? Indeed it is often a good test of any activity for me to ask if I would be prepared for others to know about it. A truly holy life is one that, when exposed, brings no shame. It is after all the secret areas of our lives that form probably the truest test of the people that we are. It is not difficult playing the saint in public, though it might not fool many. It is much harder when even the secret areas of our lives are revealed – as one day they will be.

There are drawbacks. Did anyone ever tell me of the endless arranging of chairs; the clearing out of houses that had not been cleaned or tidied for years; the tendency of even our most trusted friends to let us down when we need them most; the acrimony of some PCC meetings (though I have been very fortunate in the churches where I have served); the endless disputes about music and styles of worship; the freedom that some people feel to say what they like to you, never expecting that you might have feelings as well? 'Too much waffle, not enough worship' was one dear lady's only comment to me after I had preached one Sunday morning. The trouble was she was probably right!

I cannot complain. The ministry in which I have been involved has been somewhat specialised and seldom tedious. The pressures of city centre ministry, which has been the bulk of my work, are endlessly fascinating, and the people a constant challenge. Many clergy complain that their congregations are so slow to move. Our complaints are quite the reverse. People move on so quickly that no sooner are they trained for some area of ministry than they are off to some other church (or so one hopes!).

One thing that still at times overawes me is the overwhelming sense of privilege. By what right do I stand before people to bring God's word? Many seem to walk so much closer to the Lord than I do. Their lives bear eloquent testimony to the grace of God and yet I dare to teach them. Of course the authority is not my own, but it is humbling nonetheless.

There have been many mistakes. One recalls people upset by insensitivity, tasks left undone because one never wanted to do them, and times when one completely switched off when someone was trying to talk. Sunday evening is always a low time for me, especially if I have just preached. In fact I am usually totally incomprehensible by then. 'Remind me never to speak to him again' someone said to a friend late one Sunday night (as they admitted to me later) after they had failed to engage me in conversation.

It is all too easy to bewail the fact that a minister's mistakes are rarely forgotten, and can cause people to leave the church in disgust. But it is equally true that one little touch can mean a lot: a word of comfort to someone depressed, a word of encouragement to someone beginning in Christian leadership, even simply remembering a name after one meeting. I still blush when I recall that in the church in Paris on three successive Sundays I addressed myself to the same lady with precisely the same words 'I don't think we've met before.'

My great longing at the moment is for perseverance. One of my great heroes of the faith has always been Fraser of Lisuland. Many have been helped by his prayer of faith, but what has always struck me about him is his perseverance. Personally, I can pray with great earnestness today about something or someone, and then next week have given up. But to be a Christian minister requires hard work and perseverance. Paul spoke often of the need to be steadfast, to 'preach the word, be urgent in season and out of season, convince, rebuke and exhort, be unfailing in patience and in teaching' (2 Tim 4.2). How often have I stopped praying, or turned my attention to some other area of Christian work before God has done what he intended. Much of ministry is just hard work. But I, like so many, am always looking for the short cut, the easy way. Yet I know that there will be none. If

I am to preach a sermon that challenges and nourishes, it will only be as I give myself to study the word with real diligence. It is all too easy to be satisfied with a rehash of old material, or a superficial interpretation of a particularly familiar passage. If I am looking to see people built up, and leaders trained, it will only be because of time and effort spent in prayer and teaching. If I truly believe that it is only the gospel that makes sense of the work that we do, will I truly give myself to the work of that gospel?

Looking back I tremble, when I realise the naivety, the superficiality, and the ignorance with which I approached the ministry. But I am also deeply grateful to God, and to numerous people, for all I have received. I honestly believe that there is no work like the work of the gospel, and there is no privilege so great as to be involved in it full-time (if one can put it like that). I have many regrets as I think over my different curacies – failures, mistakes, missed opportunities, and my own sinfulness – but also a deep sense of the grace of God. 'He who calls you is faithful, and he will do it' (1 Thess 5.24).

Stephen Wookey is a curate at All Souls, Langham Place, London.

Chapter Eight

IT'S ABOUT TEAMWORK

by

Geoff Turner and Graeme Skinner

In a truly healthy society, each man would see himself as
partly responsible for the whole of it, rather than wholly
responsible for part of it

James Mathers

Graeme begins:

We turned into Church Road. We were almost there. A heartwarming sound greeted us. The church bells were ringing. What a greeting! With the children packed in the back of the car in between the luggage, with a couple of hundred miles behind us, and with three years of preparing for this moment, we had made it.

At this time we experienced a strange mixture of excitement and some apprehension. While at college we had in some way been taken out of our normal church life. You could not help being different; a bit nomadic, gathering experience as you stood back and observed (and were observed!). Horror stories had been collected and swapped of past and present curate-vicar teams. We even had a special day when clergy who were experienced came back for a flying visit, to tell us how they were getting on. 'He's a nice sort of chap and all that, but . . .' There were tales of losing days off; of the pressure on the family; of that first funeral. So what was it going to be like? Our fears and expectations focused on two specific areas: our family life, the job, and how those two related. The bells grew louder, accompanied on this occasion by the pounding of our hearts. We turned into the rectory, where we would be spending our first night, before our luggage followed us from college the next day. We had arrived.

The bells rang out with peals of joy too, for we had been looking forward to this special moment. We had been involved in Christian student work for three years before college, so were able to say that we had already experienced some of the pressures and joys of being full-time Christian workers. But this was going to be different; we were going to be able to settle into a local community at last, and we had been looking forward to that very much. We had met Geoff and Gill the year before, when we went to see the parish. Our sponsoring diocese had released us a year before the end of college. It wasn't that they were keen to see the back of us! They simply did not have enough parishes to offer to all of the ordinands they had sponsored. Earlier that year our college principal, who played an important role in placing the ordinands, had issued a questionnaire to all those who were in their final year. We filled this in carefully, giving a rough idea of the sort of parish that might be suitable for us, and stating that we would prefer to remain in the south if we had a choice. Shortly after this the principal met me in the corridor, smiled, and informed me that he knew of a parish that may well suit us; Bebington in the Wirral. Until then we had barely heard of the Wirral, all we knew for certain was that it was not in the South!

Within a couple of weeks we found ourselves heading up the motorway, keen to explore this new territory. We spent a weekend in Bebington meeting several people from the church, talking at length with Geoff and Gill, and spending time with the other clergy on the staff team. We had arrived on the Friday evening full of questions and uncertainties. We found our questions answered fully and honestly and were able to air any fears or doubts. As we drove home we hoped very much that the job would be offered to us, it would be a privilege to serve God as part of the team in Bebington. And so it was.

Geoff writes:
Graeme was about to become my thirteenth curate (never more than three at a time) a fact which I firmly told myself

had no meaning whatsoever! However, the arrival of a new colleague is a time of questioning for an incumbent just as it is for a curate. Already twelve months had passed since Graeme and Philippa and their children Hannah and Tom had spent a weekend with Gill and me in Bebington. Reports from college had been excellent and in the parish my two ordained colleagues, the churchwardens and two members of the parochial church council had all shared my feeling that Graeme should be invited to join us upon his ordination, but contact since then had been sparse. We had posted copies of PCC minutes and important news items whilst they had shared the good news of a second son's birth and of exams passed. Most helpfully Graeme had been the speaker at a parish youth weekend and consumer reaction had been, 'brill'. There was hope amongst the fourteen-year-old girls at least.

With three years as a UCCF (University and Colleges Christian Fellowship) travelling secretary behind him I knew that Graeme would already have valuable experience in preparing and giving talks and encouraging leaders of fellowship groups. But that had been before his three years at theological college. I found myself recapping the twelve who had gone before and soon realised that their attitudes rather than their abilities were what stuck in my mind. Here was the major area where my greatest hopes and fears for Graeme were to be found.

Amongst men and women recommended for training there is a common denominator of basic academic and leadership ability. Amongst UCCF travellers there is a no-nonsense belief in the divine inspiration of scripture. From his family background Graeme brought a sensitivity to people's needs and he had experience of front-line ministry. So far the bells were ringing joyously, but where was his heart? My question was not concerned with his faith in Christ, but his attitude to service in Christ's name. Peter touched on this when he wrote:

Each one should use whatever gift he has received to serve others, faithfully administering God's grace in its various forms. If anyone speaks, he should do it as one speaking the very words of God. If anyone serves, he should do it with the strength God provides, so that in all things God may be praised through Jesus Christ. To him be the glory and the power for ever and ever. Amen. (1 Pet 4.10–11)

Would the family drawing up at the Rectory door desire to serve? Was Graeme book or people oriented? Would his delight be in tapping a computer keyboard or a door-bell? I was not so naive as to think that books and keyboards cannot serve people and bring glory to God, but I did remember a former colleague for whom it was a constant struggle to remember that those things are the tools of service and not the goal.

My hope for Graeme was that he would quickly make the transition from being served to serving. Whereas in college students enjoy the priority and focus of other people serving them, once they arrive in a parish this can no longer be the case. Now they are servants serving and the minister with whom they work cannot offer them unrationed help however needful they may be.

If my first hope was to see an enthusiasm to serve Christ in his church and the parish at large my second was to welcome a brother in fellowship and friendship. It does help if you genuinely enjoy working alongside somebody, but it is not essential if you can learn of Christ and pray together. My own first curacy was spent with a man I only came to call by his Christian name years later. His life was firmly disciplined and although kindly I did not find him friendly. Each morning we prayed together, and I found in those times an assurance of fellowship and a heartening knowledge that I was working with someone from whom I could learn very much and with whom I shared a common burden in Christ's service. Could I now hope to find in Graeme the desire to share both fellowship and friendship with me, a man whose children were approximately Graeme's own age?

Inevitably for someone who has preached sermons regularly over twenty-five years there was a third hope. Would Graeme's attitudes to the people he had come to serve stretch to a genuine desire to understand them? His own experience of parish life had mostly been gained in an inner city church in London and as a student in Bristol. Bebington is a parish church not biased in any direction save that of an evangelical parish church. No age group dominates and no particular emphasis governs. We were about to embark on a reordering scheme that already threatened to become controversial both within the church and local community. What is sometimes forgotten in theological colleges and the offices of Diocesan Directors of Ordinands is the high potential for devastation inherent in some of their protégés. I hoped that in Graeme I had a man who would strive to understand the people, place and timing of his first years in the ministry. I hoped too that he would endeavour to understand both me and himself. Still the bells were ringing.

Graeme:

With the furniture in, and the children snuggled into their own allotted beds we breathed a sigh of relief. So far, so good. Geoff and Gill and all the others in the church family were being more helpful than we could have imagined. Then came the few days away, the retreat before the ordination. I knew that at home people were concerned for the family, and that was a great relief. As I processed down the aisle of Chester Cathedral on the day of my ordination, I was so pleased to see Philippa again. There was a nice touch when Bishop Michael Baughen invited all family and friends to stand up by their seats at the moment of my ordination. I was grateful that Geoff was able to be there as well. The bishop pressed his hands down on my head, prayed, and I was ordained. During the peace I was touched (squashed) by the 'peace hug' Geoff gave as he came bearing down on me. I valued that genuine gesture of Christian love. That 'little extra' will be valued for a long time to come.

Back home I felt a little strange with a white collar around my neck, perhaps it was a sort of bandage that all clergy wore after having their heads pressed down by episcopal hands! That first staff meeting, the next day, was a little overwhelming. Geoff meets with his three curates each week for two to three hours to discuss, talk and pray. I value the time immensely, although circumstances sometimes make it impossible to meet. Despite this, meeting together is a vital part of the team relationship. We discuss situations we face, and how we should progress. Once we took a series of excellent Bible studies produced by John Wimber. We tackled the Bible study together, sharing our own hopes and hurts. Spending time together, discussing the Bible and praying, soon helped us to get to know each other at a deeper level.

We also meet on Wednesday and Friday mornings at 8.30 a.m., for half an hour to study the Bible and pray. The time with God's word is very precious. It is a time when we can listen to God and learn from each other; a quiet moment before the busy day ahead. Spiritual dryness could quickly set in without times like these.

Right from the start I was given specific areas of responsibility. I was looking forward to this, after college life. The youth group and children's work was well in motion and I was aware that people were keen to find out what I would do as I arrived. Geoff was very helpful and took time to explain decisions and difficulties of previous years.

I had some experience of work with young people, but there were many aspects of the job that would be totally new. Two days after the ordination, we drove up the connecting motorway to the crematorium, where Geoff was due to take a funeral. I was doubtful about my own ability to help, even though I was to do nothing but watch! I remember the teaching technique that I was told about at college:

I do, you watch.
We do.
You do, I watch.
You do, and report back to me.

Geoff made good use of this system, and I found it most helpful. Within a couple of weeks I was launched into my first funeral. The same teaching process was set in motion with other aspects of the work. I was downing a well earned cup of tea when Geoff called me on the telephone 'A lady keeps hearing voices, and the dog keeps barking. She has asked me to come and pray in the house. Want to come?' I do not suppose anyone looks forward to their first exorcism, but together we made our way to the terraced council house, and listened to the young woman's story. Following this, Geoff prayed in the living room; kitchen; dining room; and stairs; and when we arrived on the landing he handed over the reins to me, 'Your turn Graeme.'

I have also appreciated working with someone who is aware of my limitations, as well as my strengths. At first, visiting seemed an insurmountable problem. With each weekend rushing towards me as soon as the last one finished, and with a tray full of things to be done; it seemed impossible to find time. I had been given names of people who were expecting a visit. At the end of the week I had not done them, nor at the end of the next. I had to admit the failure, and this was met with understanding.

Geoff:
Once we were into the work together I found my new deacon reassuring at every turn. Not only did he show enthusiasm but also a keenness to do things well. During the first week we visited hospitals, talked with the bereaved and shared much of the background information he required in order to work in the parish. It was agreed that Graeme would accompany me to the next church school assembly and then speak to the children himself the following week. I awaited that day eagerly and remember the confidence in my reply to a question posed in the church office later the same morning. It really had been the best talk of its type I had heard at the school. Of equal encouragement was Graeme's participation in our 8.30 a.m. fellowship times and the friendly rela-

tionships which were beginning to develop between him and members of the church family.

First talks are never easy times either for the speaker or the listening incumbent. I still grimace when Hebrews 9.13 is read in my hearing for then into my mind comes the picture of an over-zealous colleague, determined to pile on the visual aids at a family service, holding aloft a milk bottle of bull's blood and declaring that he had personally been to the abattoir to obtain it that very morning. The challenge although different can be just as keen when the first talk succeeds and is followed by more of the same. I have had two curates who have left me feeling that I have no business to be in a pulpit myself, let alone carry the responsibility of helping with the development of their preaching. On such occasions one has either to rejoice in God who gives gifts or resign. Thus far I have managed the former and was rewarded one day by hearing two strangers express the view that the vicar must be worth hearing if that was only the curate.

Relationships are greatly helped when areas of responsibility are apportioned in such a way as to maximise the strengths of individual members within a staff team. Thereby greater efficiency can be achieved and opportunities for bruising or flattering comparisons are lessened. It is also the way Christ has chosen for his body to function. A curacy is expected to provide a general training but provided that the ground is covered, each staff member can be freed for specialisation.

Graeme is now responsible for that part of the church aged from three to seventeen years. This calls into play many of the skills he developed when working with Christian Unions. The appointing, coordinating and training of leaders together with the leadership of the young people's fellowship takes up a good deal of his time. He is also responsible for the church school assembly programme and his natural talent as a cartoonist has been harnessed to provide over-head projector material for us all to use.

In Bebington we are fortunate to be able to work as a team, but more often churches have only two ordained people

working together. Inevitably that throws a greater pressure
upon their relationship and makes it even more important
that areas of responsibility are clearly defined. The first years
are for service and should not be viewed as a continuing
series of one hundred and fifty parish experience weeks.

One area of tension which arises wherever assistant ministers gather in number concerns lay leadership. I am aware
that without curates more leadership would be asked of lay
people with the probable result that the local church would
be strengthened. On the other hand lay people are rightly
given opportunities at present which minimise the experience of the clergy. Graeme could soon find himself in a first
incumbency with no other preachers and only the churchwardens to offer help with the reading of scripture during
services. He has been prepared in a general way for this to
happen but has not yet felt the weight such a ministry
imposes upon someone keen to take initiatives and perhaps
launch into a mid-week ministry programme. I well remember the shock it was to move from a well-staffed parish to my
first vicarage and face the daunting prospect of preparing
and delivering four or five different talks every week. First I
had to learn the ropes and only then did I discover how far I
could stretch in the strength God supplies.

Parish calls can soon disrupt family priorities and invade
days off and Graeme is rightly careful to guard these when-
ever possible. Certainly one day in seven is to be received as a
day of rest from the Lord, but as to the other six it behoves
ministers to remember that lay people give time to Christian
ministry after they have completed their day at work.
Furthermore we have the great privilege of eating the vast
majority of our meals with those members of our families free
to join us at home. Certainly in our experience Gill and I
have found that honouring God with our time is much like
doing so with other gifts – he is no man's debtor.

Graeme:
There was much to learn from the older more experienced
minister, but I have also enjoyed having my contribution

valued too. I have a study next to Geoff in the vast rectory.
Not long after I had arrived there was a knock at my door,
Geoff was holding a Bible in his hand, 'I'm struggling with a
sermon, got any thoughts on what this verse means?' That
did a new boy a power of good! Or last year, an hour and a
half before a sermon relating to the Armenian earthquake,
Geoff phoned with a tricky question. 'You trained as a
geologist and a theologian, what's your view on earthquakes
before the fall?' Geoff must have felt on shaky ground
(Answers on a postcard please!). I have valued this sort of
honesty tremendously. There have been times when Geoff
has been under pressure. I have learnt from his humble and
Christlike example.

Curates arrive in parishes with lots of 'Good ideas'. Ideas
and initiatives come and go. I've come up with some un-
workable ones and some useful ones. But the wisdom of
experience has not derailed me, instead I have at times been
switched to a siding, and after reflection I could see why. But
when the idea is good, Geoff has suggested that I follow it up.
Then I wish I had said nothing!

For several years, evangelicals in the Church of England
have been encouraged to become more involved in diocesan
structures. There is more to the work than your own parish
boundaries. We attend the deanery chapter meetings
regularly together. Diocesan synod never really crossed my
mind until Geoff suggested I should stand in the election.
Once on the synod, other areas of service have opened up
within the diocesan structures.

Geoff:
Graeme refers to his feelings of encouragement and they are
not restricted to his side of the working relationship. It's not
without significance that the letters of the New Testament
consistently make reference to church leaders in the plural. I
am grateful for my first four years as a lone incumbent
because the memory serves to keep me grateful for the
fellowship I now enjoy working with Graeme, Paul and
John. It helps to have others around who can share the

burden of pastoral work, but their fellowship in prayer and the wisdom and energy of mind they bring are of much greater value. Certainly the enthusiasms of the recently ordained can appear wildly inappropriate when viewed through the ten year filter of experience in a parish, but often workable ideas emerge when time is given to them. The present shapes of our house group and youth programmes are the fruits of modified curate kites and I am currently coming round to the idea of Graeme selling hot-dogs from a caravan parked outside local schools. We'll let you know!

The reordering scheme in prospect at the time of Graeme's arrival is now completed but its passage was like the wind that pushed Elijah deeper into his cave. The lay leaders within the church family were a tower of strength and so too was the support I received from Graeme. His quickness in undertaking the necessary organisation for the three day consistory court, thereby setting me free to concentrate on the proceedings, was much appreciated. Again the prayerful support of the staff team over the whole two year period of planning and change removed much of the feeling of personal strain that I would otherwise have known.

Clearly good communications must lie at the heart of any happy relationship. By the time Graeme and Philippa had reached Bebington their family numbered three small children and for obvious reasons a three-bedroomed semi did not offer the best prospect as a work base. A small room was available in the rectory and Graeme moved in. In the back of my mind was a warning I had heard years before whilst still at theological college myself. It concerned an unhappy curate whose vicar listened for his tread on the stairs and logged his comings and goings to the study he had in the vicarage attic. Not being a member of the popular Church of England's Railway Supporters' Club I decided against a programme of research into my colleague's work-shunting timetable and instead have rejoiced in the closeness of our studies. Neither bothers the other very much but the immediacy with which some things can be handled is all to our mutual advantage. My present vision is for offices for us all in a revamped hall annexe.

Graeme:
Some time before coming to the parish, I heard of a difficult situation faced by a new curate in another church. Not long after he arrived his vicar went on holiday for a couple of weeks. While the vicar was away, the new curate was invited out for a meal during which the parishioner tried subtly to undermine his confidence in his boss. Loyalty had to be learnt fast in that situation. Aware of the dangers, I came ready. Thankfully I have found a loyal congregation. Nevertheless I soon became aware that a few, a very few, dropped little remarks about decisions taken. Some suggest we are 'moving too quickly', some say 'too slowly'. It's at these points that I'm aware people are seeking to prise out my own thoughts. Loyalty counts in ministry.

Geoff:
If my first thoughts were concerned with attitudes my last have to do with the atmosphere in which Graeme and I have served together. From what has gone before you will not be surprised if I sum it up in the three words fellowship, friendship and respect. Each represents an important strand in a healthy, enjoyable and Christ-honouring staff relationship. I have hinted that friendship is not essential – the rope will not break if that cord is absent but neither of the other strands is dispensable. Without fellowship in prayer, worship and learning from the scriptures faith and vision would perish and we should become only a happy crowd of reasonably efficient caring administrators capable of a Sunday performance. Without respect for one another the enemy of all Christian relationships would strike an unerring blow aimed at confusing, dividing and spoiling Christ's body in Bebington.

It is a truism that no leader will please all the people all the time and too often a disagreement over policy, or theology, leads swiftly to rejection of the people with whom we disagree. There can be no place for papering over cracks but equally a staff team cannot indulge in the luxury of openly criticising one another or hinting at personal reservations where some decisions are concerned. Assistant ministers are valuable birds but they are birds of shorter passage than the incumbent and resident lay leaders; when all else fails they do well to accept a situation and at the same time note for the future a valuable experience in how not to do something. It is necessary to keep a sense of perspective and foolish to set everything at risk when only concerned with a five per cent issue. Likewise incumbents do well to be loyal when everyone from the local undertaker through the wedding organist to the old lady who can't hear at the back come to moan about the new arrival.

Graeme:

It's been so good to know that as a family we are valued by Geoff and Gill. They understand our needs and the pressures we face with the young family. Gill and Philippa have been out together this last year at an evening class for watercolour painting. It has been good to be both friends and work colleagues. Geoff and Gill took all of the curates and wives out for a meal one Christmas. We have laughed together; eaten together; worshipped together. We have enjoyed our time here. God has brought us to just the right place, at this time in our lives.

I wonder what the bells will sound like as we leave?

Graeme Skinner is curate at Bebington parish church, Wirral, Merseyside, Geoff Turner is rector of Bebington.

Chapter Nine

WORKING IN TANDEM

by

Susan Penfold

Wanted a curate of pious intent,
Who'll come when he's call'd, and will go where he's sent;
'Do this' the incumbent has only to say,
And the curate has nothing to do but obey

Gregory Shortcommons

The phone rings – 'Please could I speak to the Reverend Penfold?' I am sometimes tempted to reply, 'Which one?', but mostly I just pass the call on to Colin. Many of my contemporaries from theological college would be amazed at the scenario (and so would I have been in those days) – one of them found the sight of me with a 2-month-old baby amusing enough. In my days as a student I was determined not to get pushed into 'women's and children's work' – but now my major parish involvement is in Mums and Toddlers, and the Mothers' Union. So, what's changed?

I owe my call to professional ministry to my vicar, during my time as a postgraduate student in Bristol. He summoned me one day, and told me I ought to think about being a parish worker, or something similar. I'd been converted as a student in York, and had faced the challenge of giving my life to Jesus, but professional ministry had never occurred to me – I thought that was just for the super-holy. My vicar's suggestion unleashed a long chain of events which ended up with my moving to Cambridge as a UCCF travelling secretary, working with university Christian Unions, with a definite possibility in mind of applying for training as a parish worker when that job was over. It was during that time that my views on women's ministry underwent a radical transformation. Until then I had accepted the arguments about headship and authority which concluded that ordination was not appropriate for women. It was during a staff conference for travelling secretaries that I heard an exposition of 2 Timothy which really made me stop and think – and that, combined with some reflection on my role in the job I was already doing, convinced me that ordination should be open to women, and could well be my own direction.

When I arrived at Ridley Hall to train as a deaconess, I was the only female student. That caused some speculation among my friends, but I had a strong suspicion that the Lord might be calling me to remain single. I was wrong! (It is nice to be wrong, sometimes!) Colin arrived at Ridley at the same time as me, but with perhaps a more orthodox background for a potential vicar – he had been brought up in the Church of England (my early background was in the Roman Catholic Church), he had previously studied theology (I started out as a scientist), and he was interested in trains and cricket (two essential qualifications for a bishop, according to Jim Hacker's advisors). Despite all these obvious pointers, it had taken Colin a few years, and a bit of prodding by God, to get him as far as training for the ordained ministry.

It also took us several months to get past a mutual suspicion of each other's theological background, but once we got down to serious talking we realised we were both committed to biblical Christianity, rather than any particular tradition or label. We became engaged towards the end of our first year, which seemed to cause something of a stir, especially with my sponsoring diocese. 'You'll never get a job,' and, 'If this had happened sooner you wouldn't have been allowed to start training,' were two of the more memorable comments. Fortunately the college staff were supportive of our plans to marry, because to a large extent we were left on our own by our sponsoring dioceses. We managed to end up with each of them thinking we were the other's responsibility. One result of this was that when we did marry, at the end of our second year, we were left to sort out our own finances. Colin had just finished training, and was taking a year out to allow me to complete my studies, so he needed to look for a temporary job. My contribution to our joint economy was small – I still had to pay for room and board in college (albeit at a discount), and ACCM cut my grant slightly, on the grounds that a married woman need not keep up her National Insurance contributions (not that they paid them for men, anyway!). Fortunately God knew what we needed – a lovely little house at a reasonable rent appeared six months in advance, and two days before the wedding Colin got a clerical job with a department store just opening up in Cambridge.

One of the reasons we had decided to marry before I finished college, and that Colin should delay ordination for a year was to help us get used to marriage before we had to adjust to parish life. Looking back, that was undoubtedly a wise decision – and we wouldn't have wanted to wait another year to get married, anyway! It also gave us a chance to look for a job that would be right for both of us, starting at the same time – and that proved a long search. It took a while to sort out what criteria we would use in deciding which jobs to pursue.

We decided that although I did want to work full-time, we should look for only one full-time job, recognising that would probably mean that Colin would be paid, and I would be non-stipendiary (the Church pension scheme didn't seem to be able to cope with job-sharing). This was partly because we didn't want to have completely separate jobs in different parishes, which would give us little chance to operate as a couple working together, and also because we wanted to start a family and thought we ought not to wait too long (I was 31 when we married). We were prepared to look anywhere in England, and had no particular type of parish in mind, although we couldn't really see ourselves in a rural setting. We decided we would probably cope best in a parish which was broadly evangelical, and, of course, where we were likely to form a good relationship with the incumbent. But the factor which came out top every time we tried to think things through was that the parish should be one where women's ministry was welcome.

In practice we found it quite difficult to gauge incumbents' attitudes to my potential ministry. Obviously all the incumbents we talked to were prepared for me to work in some capacity, but what that might mean in practice seemed to vary widely from one parish to another. One 'test' question we began asking was whether they were prepared for deaconesses to conduct funerals – the most intriguing reply was from the incumbent who said he had no objection in principle, but that he took most of the funerals himself because people would be offended if they got the curate instead of the vicar. Was that true, I wonder? – or was it that he found taking funerals so worthwhile he didn't really want to share the job? (That's a view both of us would sympathise with – I miss them now I'm not working full-time.) Then there was the incumbent who asked Colin in great detail about his previous experience, doctrinal position and so on, but not me. I told him a bit about myself, anyway, but the next day he asked if either of us had ever been involved with the Inter-Varsity Fellowship (the old name for UCCF) – clearly he had been paying little attention to me, and neither of us was sure how to reply without embarrassing him! We also encountered an incumbent who was not prepared for me to work more than half-time, on the grounds that the rest of my time would be taken up with household chores. We said that we preferred to share the housework between us – but he said that Colin would be too busy in the parish to wash and iron his own shirts. We rapidly learnt that it was not only people's view of women's ministry which would affect our working patterns, but also their views on marriage and the roles of husband and wife within the home.

Another issue which kept cropping up as we looked at jobs was whether there was sufficient scope within the parish for two new members of staff, when the vacancy was officially for one person. In one sense there is always work for as many people as possible, but it did not always seem appropriate to have too many 'professionals'. We did come across two parishes which already had non-stipendiary deaconesses on the staff. One decided, quite rightly we felt, not to interview us. The other we visited, but felt that a parish with incumbent, two curates and two deaconesses in one church would give neither of us much scope for developing our preaching.

There were times when job-hunting seemed never-ending, and we began to wonder if we would ever find a suitable parish. We were beginning to think that two of us prepared to work was far more of a problem than an opportunity! At one stage when we were feeling particularly low I sang one of the hymns we had sung at our wedding three times in a week, and one verse seemed particularly apt:

> Fear him, ye saints, and you will then
> Have nothing else to fear;
> Make you his service your delight,
> Your wants shall be his care.

However even our job-hunting eventually came to an end, and at Petertide 1984 we were made deacon and deaconess in Chelmsford Cathedral, to serve in the parish of Buckhurst Hill. This is a very desirable area of suburbia surrounded by patches of Epping Forest, many of whose inhabitants commute into Central London each day by London Underground, which is on the surface here (!) and divides the parish into two halves. The parish is a team ministry served by three churches – St John's, the original parish church, which is at the top of the hill amongst the most expensive housing, and two former daughter churches which are 'below the line' (the Tube Central Line!). The previous curate (who had been in his second curacy) had worked mostly with the rector at the parish church, and I took over much of the work he had been doing, while Colin took on a largely new role, working with the team vicar at St Stephen's and St Elisabeth's. We did move round from church to church a bit, especially for Sunday evening services, but the parish tended to function as separate units, with some of the mother/daughter church tensions left over from the days before the team ministry. Our agreement with the parish was that we would both work full-time for a year to give us some separate experience, and that then the pattern would change. Colin would move to work in the parish church, and either I would need to take maternity leave (our first choice of options!), or we would split the work in some other way, not defined at the time.

Before we arrived in the parish we had talked through our respective roles with the rector and vicar, and attempted to carve out one area where we could work together. It was the traditional role of curates everywhere, whether it's their gift or not, 'the youth'. As the group at St Elisabeth's was lay-led and very much part of the church family there, what really needed our attention was a small, young CYFA group (which stands for Church Youth Fellowships Association), officially attached to the parish church, but drawing some of its membership from 'below the line'. In addition Colin was to function as chaplain to the cottage hospital, and to take a weekly assembly at St John's Church School, whilst I had responsibility for a weekly prayer fellowship. All this, of course, was in addition to the run-of-the-mill church activities – taking services, preaching, funerals, involvement with baptism enquiries and so on.

Things turned out rather differently from the way we expected. For various reasons, Colin didn't become involved with the CYFA group, and for several months we did very little work together. That was a disappointment at the time, although it did give us a certain amount of extra experience. It was also disastrous for the CYFA group. My experience of youth work was virtually nil (I didn't even have the experience of belonging to a group myself as a teenager), and as it turned out, my talents at coping with these youngsters were not significantly greater! There was initially no lay leadership for the group, so I was left to sink or swim. After a couple of particularly difficult incidents I did manage to find some help, but the group never really recovered from my disastrous start, and that was undoubtedly one of the factors which led to its eventual collapse.

The weekly prayer fellowship was flourishing prior to our

arrival, but had a slump in numbers as some younger members went off to college, and others were involved in running nurture groups as a follow-up to an ecumenical parish mission in the September after we arrived. These groups resulted in more people being involved in house-groups in both halves of the parish – a really exciting development which left the prayer fellowship taking some-thing of a back seat, at least for a while. We were both leading housegroups, although separately, as we rapidly realised that having both of us involved in the same group would probably stifle any possibility of lay leadership emerging.

Colin was fortunate in that in most of his work he was doing a new job, and consequently there were fewer expec-tations about how things would work out. The only roles he had inherited from our predecessor were those of acting chaplain to the cottage hospital (which closed during our time in the parish – no connection, we hope!), and a weekly assembly at the church school. He found that more difficult, as he'd been set a hard act to follow by the previous curate, and had the added disadvantage that most of the children with church connection came to St John's, so he didn't see them on Sundays.

One thing I was very nervous about when I became a deaconess was funerals. This was partly because I had never been to the funeral of anyone I knew well, and also because I had heard stories of people objecting to women conducting funerals. Initially the rector was rather cautious about me conducting funerals on my own, especially while he was away on holiday not long after our arrival. While he was away, a funeral came in for St John's half of the parish, which would normally have fallen to me. I did the visit to the next of kin, but following instructions, Colin took most of the service (fortunately not his first), including the burial in our church-yard. As he had never seen a burial there before (I had) he was relying on my instructions at various parts of the proceedings! The nicest part of this funeral was when *I* received a thank-you letter for the service – and I realised that some of our caution was unnecessary. As time went on, I began to take quite a lot of funerals, and while I made my fair share of mistakes and faux pas (like digging too hard for information on the deceased, only to discover he was chiefly known for the quantity of whisky he drank) this was an area of ministry that I found very rewarding (as also did Colin). There were occasional reservations expressed about having a woman conduct funeral services – but also a quota of very positive comments, the most amusing being on the appropriateness of my conducting the funeral of an elderly lady who was such a feminist that even her dog hated men!

When we arrived in Chelmsford diocese, post-ordination training was undergoing a major change of personnel and direction. Nothing much happened to begin with, but then in November, Colin was invited to a day for first-year clergy, but I was not. We assumed this was an oversight, since I was working full-time, and the other deaconess (stipendiary) who had been ordained with me was invited. But no – it appeared that being paid, rather than working, was the condition for invitation. Fortunately when the new 'brand' of post-ordination training (POT) was introduced in the new year, all non-stipendiary ministers (NSMs) who wished to could attend, and I eventually completed most of my first two years' POT.

In many ways that was just a minor niggle, but we did find it very hard to come to terms with the fact that although we had trained together, and we viewed our ministries as equivalent (not identical) that was not always how they were seen by others. In financial terms we were basically content to live on one stipend (we would have liked enough extra to pay someone to clean the house – but it would have been difficult to find anyone in Buckhurst Hill), but we were not happy with any links between stipend and status.

Colin's priesting was a much more traumatic event. The fine distinctions between deacon and deaconess didn't cause us much bother (apart from occasional hassles over banns certificates if the rector was away), and as we were not in a parish where most of the major services were eucharistic we had not envisaged any major change of status as a result. In the longer-term that proved true, but the fuss that was made of the occasion, and our emotional reactions to it, rather took us by surprise. I envied Colin the chance to go on retreat before the ordination. Looking back, I think I should have arranged something for myself, because it would have been good anyway to have the chance to pause for breath and reflect on my first year in parish ministry. It was also very hard to cope with people trying to make it a big occasion for Colin, when we didn't really feel that very much had changed in terms of our practical roles in the parish. But the hardest thing was that so few people seemed to realise how vulnerable I was feeling (including Colin, so he says) – or perhaps they did, but didn't know what to say. The most helpful thing that happened was when one of our lay readers asked me if I was going to go to Colin's priesting. I had seriously considered not going, but without daring to tell anyone, and it was a great relief to find someone who obviously thought this was not a silly thing to think!

Our initial plan was that I should work full-time for a year, and then we should reassess the situation. We were very keen to start a family (I was 33 by this time, and beginning to feel a bit long in the tooth!) but as we didn't seem to be making any progress on this front, it was agreed that I should carry on working. However I did try to cut down my working commitments from a six to a five day week. Tiredness was a continual problem while we were both working full-time. We did try to take proper time off. We guarded our day off jealously, even when this led to a certain amount of resentment from parishioners that we would not change it to get to their particular meeting. The problem was that even if one of us could shuffle our commitments for the week to change our free day, it was often impossible for the other to arrange to change to the same day. We did also try to find some free time each day, to stop us becoming completely workaholic, but still we were getting very tired.

Eventually we decided that the only way forward was for

me to try to keep one day a week to blitz the housework, shopping, cooking, ironing and so on, which always seemed to need doing in our free time. It was a decision we took somewhat reluctantly, as up till then we had tried to share the chores between us – a state of affairs which many of our parishioners seemed to find very odd! I was quite often asked how I was going to get the tea cooked if I was seen about the parish in the late afternoon. The reply, 'It's Colin's turn today,' drew quite a variety of interesting reactions. We would have liked to carry on like this, and both try to find extra time for chores, but felt that unless we carved out a specified day the time would simply get swallowed up in more work. The diocese had stipulated that we were not to job-share, and that Colin was to work strictly full-time, as he was receiving a stipend, so we felt that I was the only one with the flexibility to make the arrangement work. It did help to reduce the stress on us a bit, but I had not really reduced my workload only rearranged it, so I kept finding the housework day getting eroded for all sorts of other things – and it was much harder to guard than a day off!

This arrangement only lasted a few months, and then it was all change again. Colin had always known that he would eventually have to work in the parish church – my role after that move had not been defined when we started work in the parish, but we had assumed that if I were still doing a major amount of parish work when the move happened it would give us the chance to work more closely together. However it was decided that the appropriate next step was for us to swap jobs – not a decision we were very happy with for many reasons. This was one possibility that we hadn't even considered, and the decision came as quite a shock. Colin had been prepared for the move all along – I simply had never envisaged the possibility of having to start all over again at getting to know people and building new relationships after only eighteen months in the parish (the churches of the parish functioned as such separate units that neither of us knew the congregations the other was involved with in more than a superficial way). We were also intensely disappointed not to have the chance to minister among the same group of people, and find out what it was like to work together.

I was surprised at how strongly I felt – Colin had found his job much less stressful than mine (life at the parish church could be frenetically busy), and I thought I might have welcomed the change. Eventually I realised that much as I liked what I had seen of the congregations as St Stephen's and St Elisabeth's (and Colin was sorry to be leaving them), I simply had no sense at all that God was calling me to work with them. But the choice was to do that job, or not to work at all. Where was God's call – I found it very hard to tell. We eventually decided, as a compromise, that I would take over something of Colin's job, but that I would try and cut down to working half-time. It was also agreed that we would not swap housegroups – in the event we both handed on leadership to lay members of the groups within a few months, and were able to back out of those. We also found it very difficult to 'drop' one set of contacts and start on new ones, and we soon realised this wasn't entirely helpful, especially for people on the fringe of church life.

In the short time between the decision about our new patterns of working being made and our actually taking up our new jobs two significant events occurred. One was that, quite out of the blue, I was invited to apply for a temporary half-time job as a researcher with the BBC. In the end I didn't get the job, but it did confirm that perhaps we were right in thinking I should cut down to working half-time in the parish. A few weeks later I was very glad not to be commuting into central London, as we discovered I was pregnant. I was also glad not to be attempting a full workload as especially in the early stages I felt quite ill and incapable of walking any distance at all. At this stage the car spent ten days in the garage for a minor repair, and I found myself marooned at the top of the hill, feeling very remote from the congregations I was supposed to be getting to know. In the end, I worked with St Stephen's and St Elisabeth's for just under six months. It made for rather an odd period of ministry, but I did manage to put quite a lot of work into writing study material for their housegroups – a suitably sedentary occupation!

Deborah was born at the end of our second year in Buckhurst Hill, and as we lived next door to the parish church and that was where Colin spent most of his time, it seemed most appropriate and practical for us to worship there too. Perhaps my hunch that God was calling me to stay in St John's had been right, even if I did have a few very enjoyable months away. We were thrilled with our new daughter, but she brought a whole new way of life that needed quite a lot of adjustment. It felt very strange not to be involved in public ministry, and for a while I felt quite isolated at home. Having reacted quite differently to the birth of our second child, I wonder if part of the problem was that I was going through a minor bout of depression – and the adjustments weren't helped by the fact that by this time we were job-hunting again.

The question of how to combine motherhood and ministry is one that never seems to get a proper answer – every time we seem to arrive at a solution that works, circumstances change and we have to start all over again. One incident which encouraged me to think that it could be done was meeting a mum from the parish in hospital while I was in labour with Deborah. She was in some distress as her second child had died *in utero*, and she had come in to be induced. Obviously I wasn't in a position to say much at the time, but I could put her in touch with others who could help. Clearly motherhood did not preclude ministry outside the family! I did find it hard to get back to much involvement in leading services while we were in Buckhurst Hill, but as the months went by I gradually realised that between the chores of feeding and washing and nappies I was doing something very important (as well as caring for Deborah). I actually had time to *think* about what went on in the parish, and the work I'd been doing for the previous two years, and to see things I'd missed while rushing from one task to another, and this began to feed back into Colin's work, as well as my own involvement in church life. Obviously we have always

talked together about the work we've been doing (there's
plenty to talk about in church life without betraying people's
confidences) but now we were involved with the same congregation, seeing things from different perspectives, and that
was enriching for both of us.

When we came to look for our second curacy we again had to
think through the factors which would influence our choice,
and again the parish's attitude to a woman minister (I was a
deacon by this time) came out high on the list, even though
we recognised that our family life was at the stage when I
would find it hard to have much involvement in public
ministry. We also decided that we would like a change – a
parish rather more down-market than Buckhurst Hill. We
were looking for a place which would give us the opportunity
for further involvement in general parish duties, rather than
specialising in one particular area – too many parishes
seemed to want someone to do youth work. We ended up
moving to Durham diocese, to the parish of Greenside, on
the western end of the Metropolitan Borough of Gateshead.
The parish consists of two major villages, Greenside and
Crawcrook, and several smaller hamlets, all former mining
communities. There is no significant employment in the
parish now, so they are gradually turning into commuter
villages. There has been quite a lot of recent housing
development, mostly in Crawcrook, and consequently
the parish is losing some of its close-knit working-class
character.

One of our hesitations about the parish when we first
looked at the job was that it had two churches, each with
their own weekly services, as well as a fortnightly service in
the largest hamlet; we really didn't want to find ourselves as
a family torn between more than one congregation, as had
happened in Buckhurst Hill. Fortunately, this hasn't happened. As a matter of policy the parish operates as one unit,
without separate committees for each church, and the clergy
operate a weekly swap between the churches. For practical
reasons the children and I have tended to worship more often

at Greenside (mostly because we live there) but we haven't
had to decide between the two churches. Obviously there are
tensions between the two churches in the parish, and problems about transport (many people rely on buses) are not the
only factors preventing people from going to the 'other'
church when we have joint services, but on the whole the
arrangement works very well. St John's Greenside is the
original church, and the Church of the Holy Spirit, Crawcrook was formerly a daughter church, but now has the
larger congregation, and all the children's and youth work
centred there. Perhaps the reversal of fortunes makes for
easier equality.

When we first arrived we discussed our patterns of working as a staff (vicar, curate, NSM deacon). The pattern
agreed on was that Colin and the vicar would share the
workload, as had been done with the previous curate, but
that if Colin and I wanted to divide his share of preaching,
funerals etc. between us, that was up to us. I decided not to
go to staff meetings regularly – the complications over
child-minding would have been too great – but as the vicar's
and curate's families meet for lunch afterwards communications are fairly good. Most of Colin's work is run-of-the-
mill parish duties, but he is also involved with a weekly
Pathfinder Club (fortunately not as the sole leader). I didn't
want to commit myself to too much involvement in the
parish until we'd had chance to settle down, but before we
arrived I did agree to take over as enrolling member of the
Crawcrook branch of the Mothers' Union, which was facing
something of a leadership crisis. I wasn't sure how that
would fit in with caring for Deborah ($10\frac{1}{2}$ months when we
arrived), but local custom is for children to be welcome in
adult meetings (you even see them coming out of the Pen-
sioners' Club, especially in school holidays), and the only
crisis has come with the clash of meeting times as she starts at
nursery school. Recently the two MU branches in the parish
have agreed to amalgamate, thus reducing the need for
leaders (and putting me out of a job!).

Soon after we arrived a church-linked mums' and

toddlers' group, meeting in Greenside, needed a new leader, and I was asked by the members to take that on. One part of clergy life I have had quite a lot of involvement in has been preparing families for baptism, and that has made a good combination with mums and toddlers, as some of the contacts can continue on an informal level. For one reason or another I haven't shared as much of Colin's preaching or funeral work as we'd originally planned (except where I've had particular contact with the family), but we have found it very useful to cover for one another – my taking services when Colin was ill, and his helping to get mums and toddlers underway when I've been ill, or too pregnant to shift play equipment. We have gradually realised that people notice our lifestyle (Greenside village itself is fairly small – about 3,000 population), and as Christian husbands are something of a rarity we feel that even working together at that level is a joint ministry (of 'being', rather than 'doing').

When we moved we did wonder whether we would find the question of women's ordination more of an issue in Greenside than in Buckhurst Hill, as virtually all the Sunday morning services are eucharistic, which obviously restricts our opportunities to swap duties. In practice this has been less of an irritation than we had expected. The implications of having a deacon obviously hadn't occurred to the vicar – in our first weeks in the parish I discovered he had arranged for me to take a family service, followed by communion (and his theology wouldn't allow for me taking it from the reserved sacrament!). The fact that Colin is a priest and me a deacon doesn't seem to affect the attitude of the congregation to us, and we have found that in terms of church business and decisions we are both treated as *de facto* presbyters.

One aspect of joint ministry to which we have given a lot of thought has been the care of our children (we now have Deborah, aged three, and Timothy, six months). We have always been struck by the qualification for elders which states that their children should be believers (Tit 1.6), and feel that their needs must be balanced against the demands of parish life. After all, ministry happens within the home, as well as outside it, and parishioners easily become aware of when home life is going particularly badly – or well. This has meant, for instance, that we haven't felt it right to have Deborah minded too often on a Sunday morning when she was going through a clingy phase and would have been distressed to be left, even with adults she knows well. Besides, she enjoys being taken to church, and we don't suppose that will last indefinitely! We are also aware that this pattern will eventually have to change – we wouldn't want them to grow up with the stereotyped view that childcare and housework are basically for women, while men do more exciting jobs!

It hasn't always been easy to come to terms with my changing role, but I was greatly helped by a comment from a lady in the parish after a sermon on prayer, shortly after our arrival in Greenside. 'That was worth listening to,' she said. 'You know what life's like with a home to run.' It's too easy to judge professional ministry by quantity, rather than quality – most clergy seem to like being thought of as busy people – and that's probably why I found it so hard to adjust to a different pace of life. But am I now getting stuck in another rut? I hope not – but with a ministry so heavily dependent on our family circumstances, I can see that we are going to face the challenge of major changes in our working patterns and styles of ministry for many years to come. For us God's service always seems to happen among 'the changing scenes of life' (nappy-changing at the moment!). We can only wait to see how 'our wants shall be his care.'

Dr Susan Penfold is honorary parish deacon at Greenside parish, Tyne and Wear. Colin Penfold is curate at the same parish.

Chapter Ten

KEEPING AN INNER SPACE

by

Charles Read

The minister is coming down every generation nearer and nearer to the common level of the useful citizen – no oracle at all, but a man of more than average moral instincts, who if he knows anything, knows how little he knows

Oliver Wendell Holmes

Standing at the bottom of the church tower, waiting to take the next party up on the guided tour, I was approached by a lady whom I did not recognise. She obviously knew me!

'I hear you're off to university,' she said.

'Yes,' I replied, 'to read theology.'

'Theology!' she said, eyebrows raised, 'I thought you were going to be a doctor.' (I hadn't wanted to be a doctor since I was six, and I hadn't got the right 'A' levels, though people say that I've got the right handwriting for it.) 'Well,' she continued, 'you could have studied medicine and been a missionary.'

I pointed out that I was studying theology because I enjoyed it – I had no intention of being a missionary – or a clergyman! As she set off for the cream teas she offered me one last piece of advice: 'Well don't waste yourself.'

That summer fayre was one of the last events I helped with at the church where I had grown up. Shenstone is a semi-rural community in Staffordshire, a village where the church is still a focal point of many parts of village life. In the autumn of 1978 I left the leafy lanes of Staffordshire to go up to Manchester. I was reading theology because I enjoyed the subject. I had hopes of a career in university teaching and research, and I stoutly resisted people's assumptions that all theology students were going to be ordained (unless they were women, in which case they all became nuns).

During that first year at Manchester, many things changed. My firm resistance to the thought of ordination began to wobble a bit. This was largely through involvement in the university Christian Union, especially in leading part of the hall group to which I belonged.

About halfway through that first year, the vicar of Shenstone, Gordon Kuhrt, moved to Croydon. This was a cause of some sadness for me – Gordon had been a good friend and advisor. I was glad to learn that his successor was to be Robin Toley, whom I had met at Pathfinder rallies, in the West Midlands. It was when the Toleys moved into the village that I felt God's call to ministry in a different way. I offered to help them move in and, over the week or so it took to unpack boxes and move furniture, I saw vicarage life from the inside. Perhaps this was not so bad after all . . .

I returned to university and continued to get much satisfaction from involvement in the CU. I was worshipping at Holy Trinity Platt. 'Vocation' was a subject often put before the congregation there and one weekend a team came from Oak Hill college in London.

That Sunday afternoon, along with a few others, I went to the rectory to speak to the principal of Oak Hill, David Wheaton. I don't really remember much of what was said, but I do remember several people telling me, at around that time, that a good way to test a vocation to ministry is to ignore it. If it goes away, then it's just your own bright idea. If it doesn't, then it may be God's call.

I continued to enjoy university life, but this 'call' would not go away. It nagged at me, on and off, for some time. I discussed it with the rector of Platt, Hugh Silvester. I think he suggested I might push the door a little further. When I went home for the vacation, I went to see Robin 'to talk about careers in the Church of England'.

The upshot of this was that I went to see the Lichfield Diocesan Director of Ordinands. He asked me some searching questions about my prayer life, personal Bible study and how I might use my theological training in parish ministry. I did not find him at all threatening and he seemed quite satisfied with my answers to his questions.

This meeting was the turning-point. I was now officially on the books of Lichfield diocese. This raises a very import-ant point in this whole business: vocation is not just a personal matter. The inward urge was there all right, but it had come through other people (members of the CU, Robin Toley, the folk from Oak Hill and so on). *People* have always been a significant factor in my spiritual journey.

There is a theological reason for this too. We are not Christians in isolation. We are part of the church whether we like it or not. The church therefore tests our vocation. Seen in this way, selection conferences, DDOs, even bishops become part of God's way of testing our call – and not just hurdles to be overcome. In the Church of England, like most churches, you cannot just declare yourself a minister. In the ordination services of the early church, there was a section where the people could affirm the ordination of the candidates by shouting 'He is worthy!' Less exuberant, and more Angli-can, there is a similar opportunity in modern services (see ASB Ordination of Deacons, paragraph 12).

Although at first I wanted to go from university straight to theological college, I soon saw the advantages of working for a while. I know many clergy who never 'worked' before being ordained and I would never dream of saying they did the wrong thing. However, I think there are considerable advan-tages to holding down a secular job for a few years. I became a schoolteacher. Although this is often regarded as a soft option, I can assure you it is not! In such a job, you quickly see the effects of poverty, lack of attention and love in pupils' homes – and you face wider issues such as lack of adequate resources. I became quite active in my trade union, to my surprise. Apart from the general preparation which teaching gave me in terms of communication and organisational skills, it has provided me with a way into schools in my present parish. I have used my background to get alongside the staff and I find that I have been accepted by them as one who can sympathise with their problems.

This raises another important theological point. Training for ministry does not begin when you start college. God has been preparing you for years. It is perhaps only later on that you see this. One of the things I learned at university was that there is more than one way to be a Christian. I came from a fairly conservative evangelical background and expected to be involved in the CU, but not in chapel activities – after all, they were all liberals or catholics. To my surprise, nearly all the members of my hall CU group went to chapel on Wednesday evenings. I dutifully went too. It was a eucharist, somewhat higher than I was used to, but, as I went along each week, I began to appreciate this style of simple catholic worship. I got to know the chaplain fairly well. To my surprise he was a Christian even though he was an anglo-catholic! This seems silly and obvious looking back now, years hence, but it was a major revelation then.

Similar surprises awaited me on my course. I had come up to university armed with all the right answers to questions I might meet studying theology. I knew all the arguments in favour of Moses writing the entire Pentateuch; I could demonstrate at length the historical trustworthiness of the Gospels, and so on.

My initial shock was that I *was* disturbed by intellectual problems – even though I thought I had read up all the right evangelical answers! I remember that the biggest problem for me in that first year was the way in which Paul uses the Old Testament in his epistles – in a way which no one would use the OT nowadays! I still haven't got any watertight answers to *that* question.

However, all these wicked liberals who teach theology in our universities turned out to be very pleasant people. More than that, most of them *were* Christians. They did not all hold the evangelical beliefs I did, but they certainly knew the Lord. I sometimes heard some of my lecturers preach and I can honestly say that they preached more stimulating, biblically-based sermons than I have often heard from evangelicals.

So God was demolishing my prejudices against liberals and catholics. I have found my own beliefs becoming more open over the years while my belief in the centrality of the cross, the Trinity and the incarnation has become stronger and stronger. While I have remained an evangelical at heart, I have learned much from Christians of other traditions. My vision of God has been enlarged.

This is all very important for future Anglican clergy. We belong to the Church of England and not just to one part of it. We need to learn from each other, to listen to each other and to work together. Like it or not, the Church of England is a comprehensive church, catholic *and* reformed. This does not mean being uncritical of other Christian traditions, but it does first of all mean being willing to listen and to learn.

The 'itchy feet' syndrome would not go away. While teaching I trained as a Reader and so got some experience of preaching and leading worship. I went to see the DDO again – this time in Manchester diocese. I had got engaged three days before seeing him and this was a wise move, for questions of marriage need always to be discussed with your bishop and DDO once you have begun your formal route to ordination. Judith and I have been pleased that all my interviews in the diocese were open to both of us. The question of the role of a clergy wife is rather difficult and complicated.

Perhaps the traditional role makes a wife (or husband) into an unpaid curate. A curate's wife is expected to run the Mothers' Union and/or young wives group, bake endlessly for the church bazaar and always be in to take messages, make cups of tea for callers and so forth. The assumption is that she has no job outside the home and church.

Nowadays, most clergy wives do have a paid job, at least part-time, unless they have very small children. A swing away from the traditional role model can result in a curate's wife having *nothing* to do in the life of the parish. This too can be a real problem, especially if she is used to being active in church work. Her husband has a defined role and specific jobs to do. The parish is so keen not to cast her into the traditional mould that she is effectively ignored.

The problem with both extremes is that it ignores the wishes of the individual wife. *She* should be consulted herself! It is impossible to lay down what is right in this area. Each parish must display sensitivity so that the new curate's wife is not overburdened, put upon or ignored.

After two fairly laid-back interviews with the DDO, I was sent to see an examining chaplain. The examining chaplain was a vicar in Ashton-under-Lyne who asked me to define my concept of ministry. We spent the best part of three hours in deep theological discussion. At one point he asked Judith what *her* theological background was. She replied: 'Well, Albert, what exactly do you mean?' That is the kind of answer a true theologian gives!

This interview may sound daunting – but remember it was intended for someone with a degree in theology. The aim of the interviewing process is to build up a picture of the candidate, not to trip you up.

There was some delay in getting a date for a Selection Conference (usually called, wrongly, an ACCM conference). I cautiously reminded the DDO that he had promised to fix one up for me and he dutifully apologised that wires had got crossed and I would not be able to start college (if I were recommended) for another year. A set-back and disappointment, but it did mean we spent our first year of marriage in Manchester rather than getting married and moving all in the same summer. The thing to remember is that the ball is nearly always left in your court. The DDO will not chase you – *you* have to ask for further interviews, and so on.

Eventually I went to a Selection Conference (in March 1986) at Morely in Derbyshire. Many people dread these conferences. I think all of us at this conference enjoyed ourselves immensely. There was a great variety among the six selectors: two women, three lay people, two evangelicals, three from the north and so on. The atmosphere was very relaxed. One evening we all got together and sang choruses – the amazing thing being that the evangelicals and the anglo-catholics knew the same ones – we had all been touched in some way by the charismatic renewal movement. This movement seems to have had a far greater effect on the church than many people realise – but that's another story!

The result of the conference came through very quickly. I was recommended for training. (It is important to realise that the conference does not recommend anyone for *ordination*.)

So in September 1986 we moved to Nottingham, a return for me to the leafy lanes of the Midlands. For Judith, it was the first time she had lived anywhere but in Manchester.

There is some criticism of the whole idea of residential training at present, but it does have the advantages of being intensive and of offering the student the chance to live in some form of Christian community for a while. But this type of theological education can foster the idea that the college experience is the sole training for ministry. Training starts much earlier on and it should continue for all your life.

In some ways, St John's was disappointing. I expected it to be full of dynamic people with lots of good ideas for ministry. In fact the other students were just like me – very ordinary. Some students even struck us as rather naive. Then I remember something Hugh Silvester had said to me years ago: when a person is first at theological college, they quickly see the faults and shortcomings of other students and wonder if they ought to be heading for ordination. After a while, they begin to see their own inadequacies and wonder if *they* are suitable for ordination. There is a third stage: realising that God accepts you as you are and has called you as you are to serve him.

In fact I did learn a lot from other students at St John's. More theology is done in the common rooms of colleges than in lecture theatres. Learning from other people is a vital skill for ministry. We are not called to go it alone. We made many friends who were very supportive in difficult times (especially illness and when we were looking for a curacy). People did not always see eye to eye, but learning to handle disagreements and growing through conflict is part of growing as a Christian.

I studied ethics, biblical texts, preaching and pastoralia (which is not Italian cooking, but very useful all the same).

Practical placements are an important part of the college training period. The first thing I had to do was to go on sermon classes. About ten students and a tutor go to a different church each week. One of you preaches and afterwards there is a discussion of the sermon, often with members of the congregation as well as the sermon class. This appears a daunting prospect at first. Two things struck me. First, the high standard of preaching from the other students. Second, everyone was keen to be helpful and not destructive. Comments on sermons were constructively critical. The drawback to this whole system is that you are preaching to a congregation you know nothing about and may never see again. However, when someone says to you afterwards that God spoke to them through your sermon, you really do know that the Holy Spirit is at work! Visiting different churches in this way is also a good way of seeing something of the breadth of the Church of England. This can be something of a shock for people who have only ever worshipped in one church or one sort of church. You can see God at work in unexpected ways.

Let me give an example of this. There is one church in the East Midlands which has a dreadful reputation. Horror stories about it from students on sermons classes abound – how the organist begins the next hymn if he thinks you should have finished preaching and so on. When we went there, the girl who was preaching had prepared a short sermon, having been told ten minutes was the absolute maximum length. During the hymns, the vicar chatted away to the people on the front row. Seven minutes into Mandy's sermon, the organist played a very loud note on the organ and began shuffling his music! By the end of the service we all felt thoroughly fed up with the whole performance. Was there any spiritual life in this church at all? Then several members of the congregation invited us to the church-warden's house for a prayer and praise meeting. Here was a sign of hope! Of course, this raises all kinds of questions about what is 'real' worship but that evening many of us learned (yet again) not to be too judgemental about churches.

Colleges also often arrange secular placements. You may do one or two of these, depending on how long your college course is. I spent a fortnight on a media project, finding out about local radio and tv. We visited radio and tv stations and made a short video. All of us who took part in this project found it fascinating and for many of us the media bug bit. There are a surprising number of ways in which local clergy can be involved in local media.

My final year church placement was at St Augustine's Derby. I spent all of September working in the parish and then went in each Sunday and for one other day each week. Both Judith and I thoroughly enjoyed our time there. The placement was supposed to finish at Easter of my final year but we continued to worship there until we left Nottingham.

The success of this placement shows, I think, why some curacies work out well and others do not. One of the key factors is personal relationships, especially with your vicar. Mike, the vicar, and I got on very well almost from the start. Judith and Ruth (Mike's wife) also became friends. Mike and I found we had a number of things in common and this undoubtedly helped to make my working in the parish fairly easy.

I was also trusted to get on with things on my own. A student on placement cannot realistically be given major areas of responsibility in the life of the church. However, being able to let the student get on with tasks unsupervised and then to have them report back is a good way of expressing trust in that student and making them feel they have something to offer.

Mike was always willing to discuss what I had been doing and this theological reflection was an important part of what I did in Derby. The discussion was not just about what I had done and how successful it had been, but also, and most importantly, was concerned with the theological issues involved.

'Theological reflection' is a term bandied about in all sorts of ways in colleges. People seem at a loss to define it. Yet it is not some great secret. All it means is that pastoral situations have a theological side to them which is the key to them. So, for example, if you are talking to someone who has come to see you, the key element is not 'What advice shall I give to this person?' but 'What is God doing in this person's life?' Or, to give another example, if a church is short of money, the question is not 'How do we raise money/increase giving?' but 'What is happening *spiritually* here (in this financial crisis)?'

Theological reflection uses the knowledge, skills and insights acquired in the study of the Bible, doctrine, church history and soon in a pastoral context. In other words, it seeks to integrate pastoral and academic. It stops your ministry being entirely pragmatic, asking what can I do to rescue this situation (when things go wrong) or how can I maintain this situation (when things are good). Fundamentally, it asks basic questions about God and what he wants in a church (or some other context). Its operation depends on the minister continuing to think and to reflect after leaving college.

It has been observed that theological reflection is best done in groups. This is why a good relationship with your vicar is important – you need to be able to talk theologically with him and he needs to be able to listen to your wild ideas!

One final word on this very important topic is to say that it is not a clergy preserve. We should be helping our congregation to relate their faith to the situations they find themselves in.

Towards the end of your time at college, the time comes to look for a curacy. When going to look at a prospective parish, it is a good idea to draw up a list of questions to ask and things to look for. You must attend some Sunday worship and also see the curate's accommodation. You need to take into account the needs of your family as well as your own enthusiasm (or lack of it) for what is on offer.

The vicar needs to be someone who can train you and with whom you can talk. This does not mean you are going to be great pals with him from the first day. Friendships take time to develop. Most parishes offer good training possibilities, but not all vicars are good trainers. Perhaps one day *all* dioceses will employ a system whereby an incumbent gets a curate only if he *is* a good trainer (some dioceses have begun to do this already).

The parish needs to decide if they want to invite you to be the new curate and you need to decide if you want to go there. Again, it is to be hoped that incumbents will employ lay people in making their side of the decision. If both sides agree it is right then your search is over!

There is no virtue in being over-fussy in what you look for in a curacy parish, but likewise you need to be able to say no if a place is not right. We looked at four parishes altogether and a friend of ours looked at fourteen! Of our four parishes, we were very keen to go to the first one and everyone thought we would be offered the curacy. We were not. We were shattered – this parish seemed so wonderful! We later came to terms with this and we now get on very well with the incumbent who turned us down.

After looking at three parishes and still not having got ourselves fixed-up, we were asked to go and see the bishop – just to see if anything was wrong. We found then and throughout our time at college (and beyond) that the diocese was very supportive and caring. People often see the bishop and his officers as 'them' – a hurdle to be jumped – but we have never found this. I think it is very important to see the diocesan structures and officials as part of God's system of guidance and help for us.

When we met with the bishop, the DDO asked me a rather strange question.

'Just how evangelical are you?' he said.

'Well,' I replied, 'it depends on what day of the week it is!'

'Would you consider looking at a non-evangelical parish?' he continued. We replied that we would look at any parish on its merits. My convictions about evangelicals needing to be part of the whole church, catholic, liberal and all, were being put to the test. It is one thing to say that you believe we all have a part to play, it is quite another to go and work with Christians of another tradition!

In the end, we went to look at a parish in a small town in our diocese, a town centre team ministry where the churchmanship was somewhat catholic. We went to a Sunday morning eucharist and after watching the way in which worship was conducted, with a fair amount of ceremonial, Judith asked me if I could cope. I thought I could. The vicar seemed a pleasant sort of person and the congregation was friendly. Eventually I was offered the curacy there and I accepted it. On July 3rd 1988 I was ordained deacon and began my ministry in this parish. If anyone had told me, twelve months earlier, where we would end up, I never would have believed them! God moves in mysterious ways.

Other curates who, like me, were evangelicals working in non-evangelical churches, had said that this makes you more of an evangelical than you were before. I soon began to see what they meant. At an evangelical college like St John's you easily question your evangelical heritage – the fact you are surrounded by people who generally think the same way as you, gives you the support and freedom to do this. The challenge of working in a different kind of theological environment makes you ask why you react against certain things (prayer for the dead was one example in my case) and also makes you think out more clearly why you believe and do certain things.

Much of the worship at St Mary's (and the other two churches in our team) helped me to meet God. There were things I found more difficult. Prayer for the dead (in the sense of trying to alter their fate after death) I found unacceptable and I prayed instead for the bereaved family, commending the person who had died to God's care and mercy (which is what we do in the funeral service anyway).

In a situation of this kind, it is important to be able to
discuss issues with your vicar, or other members of the staff
team. Our team consisted of three evangelicals and three
anglo-catholics. Our weekly staff lunch was a time for discussion. We need to remember we do not have all the
answers. There is a need to listen and to try to understand.
It is also wise (and encouraging) to find common ground.
For example, while we found we had different understandings of what the eucharist was about, we agreed on the
atonement.

An important side of this parish's life was its civic func-
tions. We hosted such things as the mayor-making service
and the Remembrance Day service. Sometimes we felt used –
services were presented to us to lead which we could not
agree with all they contained. Some groups wanted to sing
the hymn *O Valiant Hearts*, which includes references to death
in war as being 'lesser Calvaries' and like the death of Jesus.
We never really faced this conflict with what is expected of us
by such groups. We wanted to take some sort of stand on the
truth as we saw it and yet we did not want to lose the contacts
we had with these groups. If we appeared to be rejecting
them, they may well have felt that God was rejecting them.
(Clergy face a similar dilemma over baptism requests.)

Curates will often feel frustrated because they cannot do
things their own way. St Mary's baptism policy was to
baptise all comers. There was no baptism preparation at all
and I began to visit baptism families prior to the baptism, to
talk to them about the service. As a curate, I had no
authority to change this policy or pattern whereas given a
free hand, I would have introduced the system we had at St
Augustine's Derby, which seemed to work very satisfac-
torily. There, everyone who asked for baptism for their
children was offered a service of thanksgiving first. After this
service (which was offered unconditionally), baptism could
be discussed. The 'thanksgiving first' pattern seems to me to
be advantageous because it meets the pastoral need to do
something for a new baby, a need felt by many parents, most
of whom cannot put it into words, but it also prevents

baptism becoming a thanksgiving for the birth of a child. Baptism is thus given its proper status as an initiation rite.

Alongside the frustrations, there are unexpected joys. A common evangelical problem is to assume that God is not active in non-evangelical churches. A common curate's problem is to assume that God has not been active in the church they are going to until they arrive! To my surprise and delight, I found a lot of evidence of God being active in St Mary's long before I went there.

One evening, we were going on a coach to a Mothers' Union rally in Manchester. I could not help overhearing the conversation from the two ladies sitting behind me. One of them was saying that her marriage had changed since her husband had started coming to church with her. Previously, he used to come home from work, have tea and spend the rest of the night in front of the tv. Now he was helping with cubs and scouts and they actually talked to each other! The thing that annoyed him most, she said, was when their son went into their bedroom, read his father's Bible which was on the bedside table, and lost the place in it! No-one had ever told this man he ought to read his Bible every day, but he just did it. I listened to this story in amazement and was struck again at how God works in spite of us as well as through us.

Similarly, we had heard for years of how you ought to try to bring friends to church. We had seldom seen it done outside student circles. At St Mary's people were quite good at it! No one had ever told them they ought to do it – they just did. We quickly found that there was also a demand from the congregation for housegroups, a church bookstall and a weekly news/prayer sheet. What struck me was that I knew of many clergy who were labouring long and hard to introduce homegroups and finding it hard to convince people of their worth, while here we were in a parish with a congregation almost clamouring for such things!

One of the most unsupervised jobs in the world is that of the Anglican clergyman. Therefore you need some self-discipline and some means of organisation. You sometimes hear of lazy clergy – most of whom are probably just disorganised. I try to plan a day's work each morning. At St Mary's I would begin by meeting my vicar to say Morning Prayer – this at least has the merit of making you pray and read the Bible at the start of a busy day. Mornings were often spent in preparation, dealing with post and so on. It is vital to prepare things adequately. This is true of sermons and teaching activities or meetings but it is also important to plan visiting, so you do not end up travelling miles to see people.

I kept a list of people I visited who were more or less confined to home and noted when I visited them – so there wasn't too long a gap between visits. When my vicar came to the church (a year before I did), there were no records of any kind about visiting, so we had to start from scratch. This meant that we often got complaints about 'the clergy not visiting' someone – but we could not visit someone we did not know existed! We kept a card index of people in the vestry and recorded our visits on this. Some such means of organisation is vital. We got the congregation to fill in some of these cards with their own names and addresses and I would often pick a few people out of the card system to visit during a week. This means you are visiting your congregation fairly systematically and not just doing crisis visiting (if someone is ill) or business visiting (e.g. for a baptism enquiry).

Meetings slotted into this pattern – or rather the desk work and the visiting were fitted around the meetings! Our diocese recommends that clergy divide the day into three and work no more than two of these parts each day, while also taking one full day off each week. It is easy to fall into the trap of working all your waking hours, and indeed some clergy will imply you are lazy if you do not! Clergy guilt is a major problem. You feel you *ought* to be doing more – you shouldn't be taking time off. Married clergy can overcome this by ensuring that they spend time with their family. Single clergy may need some encouragement from their friends and congregation. Ideally, the vicar ought to be doing this, but it is difficult if your vicar is a workaholic himself! However, if you do not rest properly (and that means taking some time off each day) then you will get tired quickly and you cannot be effective if you are tired out.

This takes us back to what I said earlier about theological reflection. If you fill your time with activity and end up rushing around being busy, then you will look as if you are achieving a lot. In fact, you may be achieving very little. There needs to be time for study and reflection. You may want to take a study morning each week, or to do a small amount of Bible study each day. I tend to study something as a topic. Recently, I had to preach on Jesus' teaching on marriage and divorce (in Mark 10). Several of our congregation are divorced and people had often asked me about the church's stand on remarriage of divorcees. So I set about doing some fairly systematic study of all this (we had only managed to look at the subject briefly at college). Some of what I studied went into the sermon (especially the work I did on the biblical texts). The rest of it has informed me generally and helped me to think more deeply about this subject – so I can help people in the parish who ask me about it.

Apart from study of this kind, it is very useful to ask yourself what God is doing (or wants to do) in your parish! You cannot do this with every item in your diary, every meeting, every visit, but you can reflect in this way on some items. What is God doing in the lives of the married couple I wrote about earlier? Where is God in the midst of our financial crisis? This kind of task is vital if the 'desk' sort of studying is to relate to your everyday pastoral work and if your ministry is to be theological rather than merely pragmatic. (That is, if you want to see what God's vision for your situation might be, rather than merely maintaining what is there or solving problems as they arise.)

The following have helped me to keep thinking:

1. Post ordination training, chapter meetings and the like all provide opportunities for input and discussion.
2. Keeping up with some reading. I try to set aside a little time each day for this and subscribe to Grove Books,

which I find are very useful for getting to grips with a subject quickly. I read the *Church Times* and the *Church of England Newspaper* and try to read a local paper and watch the news each evening.

What happens if it all goes horribly wrong? One of the reasons I was asked to contribute to this book was that I had some difficulties in my curacy. I was going to write that it had not been a particularly happy curacy – but that would have been wrong. There were many times when it was a joy to see God at work in people's lives and there were many things I did which I greatly enjoyed doing.

However, things did go wrong. I am writing this too close to the events to go into the details of the situation, but, suffice it to say that my relationship with my incumbent was not very good. I was unsure if this was simply because I was a young man full of his own ideas who needed to settle down into ministry. After a few months, Judith and I decided to talk to the vicar of our neighbouring parish. We had known this man for years – he had been a curate at Platt years ago. We found it was a tremendous release just to talk to someone about the problems we were having and he in turn contacted the DDO to ask 'what a chap does if he's having trouble getting on with his vicar'. The DDO's reply was that the chap goes to see him!

I went to see our DDO, still feeling that the problems may be entirely of my own imagining. During that and subsequent visits, it became clear that there were real problems to be faced. The DDO spent a lot of time talking to us and helping us to analyse the situation. I tried talking to my vicar about it all, as did the DDO. Somehow we found it hard to make any progress. Eventually, I had to see the bishop. This was a routine interview, just prior to my being ordained priest. We talked for a long time about what had gone wrong but I came away not feeling much wiser about what to do. At the retreat just before the ordination weekend, I spoke to our DDO again. This was like a cloud lifting and the sunlight streaming in! The diocese had decided that I could finish my curacy after two years and move to another job in the diocese. There was light at the end of the tunnel! Meanwhile, I was to keep in touch with the DDO – he felt it was vital that I was not isolated in the parish.

Different dioceses have different ways of dealing with problems like these. I suspect most curates feel as I did that they are alone with their difficulties – the diocese will always back up their incumbent! I have found that to be untrue. The diocese wants to help. Someone like the DDO (or your archdeacon) can mediate in a difficult situation. Evangelicals are often suspicious of the powers that be, but we need not be.

There is a spiritual dimension to all this too. When things were particularly bleak, we found ourselves asking 'Why did God send us here?' You begin to wonder if God has abandoned you, or played some cruel joke on you. Such experiences throw you back on God's resources, which is no bad thing in ministry – we can begin to think we are doing it all.

Not long after I went to St Mary's, I had to take the funeral of a 22-year-old who had died of Cystic Fibrosis. The family and friends were understandably distraught. I remember preaching at the funeral about being able to get angry with God and how God knows about suffering because Jesus suffered. (I had learned this from the work of a German theologian, Jürgen Moltmann, and this is a good example of using theology in pastoral ministry, even if I say so myself!) Similarly, Jesus was misunderstood and his ministry was rejected. Such ideas can sustain us when ministry is difficult. It is perfectly possible to be angry with God for putting you in a difficult parish. God can take your anger and frustrations and still love you!

I wrote earlier of how people have been significant for me in my Christian pilgrimage. So too, when the curacy became difficult, I found the support of others invaluable. My POT tutor group was especially helpful. Here I could unburden myself in confidence. (You cannot talk to parishioners about such difficulties – come what may, you must be loyal to your incumbent.) Other friends outside the diocese were also very supportive in listening to our story and praying for us. The moral is that if it is important to keep on thinking and reflecting after ordination, it is all important to have a support network of some kind. You may have a cell group which meets a few times a year to pray for each other. You may have a spiritual adviser with whom you can discuss your own spiritual life. You need something to help you as you help others.

Charles Read is now curate at St Clement's, Urmston.

POSTSCRIPT

by

John Martin

John Martin is the editor of the *Church of England Newspaper*

Dear Matthew

I was glad to hear your news that your long search for a post is over and that very soon you will be a fully paid-up curate of the Church of England. People from St Michael's are planning to turn out in force for your ordination. It will be a special moment for those of us who have followed your progress in the faith since you were a young shaver!

It has been great to have kept in regular touch by letter since you went to college and I was wondering if we might make 'ministry in the early years' our main topic over the next few months. You must tell me if I get too pompous or boring. My best hope is that my layman's contributions will be like the Curate's Egg – good in parts.

I read the other day that Britain is now regarded as the most 'pagan' society in Europe with 43 per cent of the population claiming no religious beliefs whatever. In my worst moments I wonder if the same thing is happening here in Britain as happened to the church in North Africa. In the days of St Augustine of Hippo the church there was strong and vibrant. Over relatively few decades it disappeared without a trace.

The biggest factor in its death was loss of vision. One of our greatest problems in the church founded by the other Augustine is our pessimism that the forces of secularisation and the erosion of belief in our community can't be beaten. In so many places there is talk of retrenchment and decline as if they are inevitable. That is to under-estimate the power of the Good News of which the church is both guardian and herald. My wish for you is that you will have your own special place among a new generation of biblically-inspired leaders who will – in the words of John Stott – 'rip the mask off the face of our secularised western culture and reveal its bankruptcy.'

I am certain about one thing. As much as I welcome all the innovations we have seen in the forms of ministry in the church in recent years – non-stipendiary ministry, the local ordained ministry, and all the rest – more than anything else we are going to need to recruit a lot of high calibre young people like you who will give the best years of their lives to full time ministry.

As you begin your ministry I think I can do no better than sum up all my prayers for you in Paul's words to the young Timothy: 'I remind you to re-kindle the gift of God that is within you through the laying on of my hands; for God did not give us a spirit of timidity but a spirit of power and love and self-control' (2 Tim 1.6–7).

*   *   *

Dear Matthew

I am not at all surprised to hear you say that you feel a bit 'down' after all that has happened over the past few weeks. People tend to forget that clergy are as human as the rest of us. You need to recognise that all the recent events in your life – leaving college, getting married, moving house and taking on a new job – all add up to a tremendous amount of stress.

In my job I meet a lot of clergy. There seems to me to be a big problem with over-work and stress. Perhaps it's the fact that most live 'over the shop' and feel on call all the time. I often wonder as I see a sweating clergyman arriving late for meetings, profusely apologising because their last meeting 'went on a bit' and sinking into a chair in exhaustion, what is really being achieved with all this frenetic activity.

A minister who recognises stress in himself and others has a lot to offer. I found it helpful to read about the work of Dr Thomas Holmes who developed a 'life change chart' which assesses how much stress you are under. He assigned points for events that cause stress. He says that accumulating over 200 a year signals a need to take care. Death of a spouse is one of the most stressful (100 points). So is losing your job (47). Even Christmas with all the rush and family reunions is stressful (13 points according to Dr Holmes). All the recent changes in your life add up.

I am not saying that we should not work hard. To achieve anything worthwhile needs a lot of hard slog and determination. What is more, none of us is paced exactly the same way. Some of us naturally work harder and play harder than others. And we need a certain amount of stress to keep us on the boil. But the point is the way in which that energy is *directed*.

The point is to have a sense of *focus*. Here's a subject for Bible study on a wet Sunday afternoon. The Bible doesn't actually use the term, but the idea is there. St Paul knew lots about it. In Philippians 3.13 he says: 'One thing I do. Forgetting what lies behind and straining forward to what lies ahead, I press on towards the goal for the prize of the upward call of God in Christ Jesus.' Paying attention to the idea of *focus* has been at the heart of many of the spectacular 'turn-rounds' of ailing businesses over recent time. John Harvey-Jones, the former chairman of ICI, wrote recently that one of the secrets of his success in re-vitalising the company was that he made sure that every single person in the operation had a clearly defined, single objective and devoted all their working energy to pursuing it. Harry Emerson Fosdick once said: 'No steam or gas ever drives anything until it is confined. No Niagara ever turns into light and power until it is tunnelled. No life ever grows until it is focussed, dedicated and disciplined.'

There will be many times in your ministry when you feel a

'bit down' – or even worse. The great Spurgeon once said that a sure recipe to beat spiritual dryness was to have a good holiday. Some people find that sports or jogging helps. Being disciplined about your diary and taking proper days off will help too. You will need to protect quality time with Ruth. But most important is being able to draw on inner resources.

Parish life rarely enhances the spiritual lives of the clergy – it drains them. The key to overcoming stress and avoiding burnout is to make certain that among all the demands, you don't allow time for keeping your own spiritual life fresh to be eroded away.

*   *   *

Dear Matthew

You have asked for my thoughts on the ministry itself. A big problem with the church today is that it's not all that sure what the job actually is. I remember the Archbishop of Canterbury recently telling the General Synod: 'When we talk about the ordination of women, one of our problems is that we are not all that sure what it is we are actually putting them in.'

As we all know, the job has changed radically in the last century. The vicarage used to be very important in the social order. It was the hub for most of the relief and welfare work that went on in the community. It controlled the local school. It was often the only source of medical advice (one of the most popular medical 'texts' being a work of John Wesley). Clergy were the leaders of the community because as often as not they were the only educated people on hand.

Now most of that has changed. The role of the clergy has been 'slimmed down'. And there are too many clergy who try to deal with their own uncertainty about the nature of the job by using all kinds of ingenious ploys to inject themselves into all sorts of causes that don't particularly need them. You know the story of the clergyman who made the point of being down by the railway track when the daily train came through the village. Asked why, he said, 'This is the only thing I don't have to push in this town.'

The curate's job has changed as well. Forty years ago the average curate in his first post was 22 or 23 and single. He would have gone to theological training straight out of college or university and would be ordained 'on potential'. He would in all probability have been a part of a team of up to six curates. He would have done at least two curacies before taking an incumbency. He was normally very wet behind the ears and his vicar would keep an eagle eye on him.

Now the average curate is 28, married, and – like yourself – is already an articulate and recognised Christian leader having done lots of important jobs in the home parish before going to theological college. There are hardly any second curate's posts, so all being well, in about three years time you will be looking out for a parish of your own.

That implies an entirely different relationship between curates and vicars than before. The first curacy, according to the powers that be, is still seen as an extension of the training process. But the dynamics can be very different. For people who are as experienced and articulate as you, it will not seem fair if your vicar reserves the right to criticise your sermons without putting himself on the line as well.

I know a lot of horror stories about this relationship going wrong. Let me tell you just one. Bill was a vicar of a few years standing. He knew David who was a mature-age ordinand and was delighted to have him as his curate. Trouble began when David went to a renewal conference and came back inspired. He had always considered Bill to be a bit conservative. David would have said that it was just a coincidence that there was soon a group of about sixty coming to the curate's house on Tuesdays for prayer and praise. Soon the whole parish was divided into two factions, each centring around the personalities of the two clergy.

It is your vicar's parish, not yours. You no doubt will have lots of ideas. But you are the temporary factor. It's down to you to honour Graham and be loyal even when that grates on you – especially when discontented people come around trying to enlist you as their ally.

*   *   *

Dear Matthew

I deserved your response to my last letter. Here I was going on about the ministry as if it was the sole prerogative of the clergy. I of all people should have known better.

When we talk about the ministry we need to start with the biblical idea of the call of God. There are two dimensions:

1. All Christians are called. We have been called 'out of darkness into God's marvellous light' (1 Pet 2.9). We have been called to be his covenant people, to be members of the community of the church. We have been called to regard our daily work as something which is to be done 'as unto the Lord'.

2. Then the Bible and the history of the church tell us that God calls and equips people for particular tasks in his service. The Bible is full of stories of how God called people to do his work. And he gave them the necessary gifts (charisms) of grace to do the job.

When it comes to the ordained ministry of the Church of England it is interesting to notice the big difference between our practice and that of the early church. These days the idea of having a 'call' seems to be very much an individual thing. As editor of *The Church of England Newspaper* I get a lot of letters from people expressing indignation: they *know* God has called them. How dare the Church of England turn them down!

In the early church the system worked in the opposite way. It was the church community that made up its mind that Fred or Jane should be appointed to serve in a particular task. It took a very strong-minded individual to resist that kind of call. The 'inner' sense of calling would have come later from successfully doing the job.

Another contrast is that under our present system, when an individual's sense of call is recognised and affirmed by the wider church, the person concerned leaves the community in which the call and gifts were first recognised and is sent somewhere else. Not surprisingly most candidates for ordination in the Church of England come from 'lively' parishes. The first weeks in the 'average' parish can be quite a shock to the system!

The clergy have a special task to enable and focus the ministry of the whole people who have responded to the call of God. It is a calling to a special form of leadership – leadership that seeks to bring out and develop the gifts of the other 99 per cent of the church.

The church could take a leaf out of the book of Sir John Harvey-Jones who said of his role in ICI: 'I am not the proprietor, not dominant. I lead by example and by persuasion and a lot of hard work. Not on the basis of power or authority. My skills are to help a large number of people to release their energies and focus themselves. It is switching on a lot of people and helping them to share a common aim. People only do things they are convinced about. One has to create conditions in which people will want to give their best.'

Another of my favourite quotes about leadership comes from a fourth century Taoist called Lao Tzu:

> Of the good leader . . .
> when his task is accomplished, his work done
> The people say, 'We did it ourselves'.

The Church of England does not have a job description for the clergy. But at least it is working on it. ACCM (the Advisory Council for the Church's Ministry) described the central core of the role of the clergy under three headings:

- Keeping alive the faith of the church;
- Proclaiming the mystery of God;
- Engaging with the world.

I doubt I would want to use this sort of language. But this is very helpful.

1. Keeping alive the faith of the church is one of the big issues of our times. For my part I was brought up in a section of the church that was suspicious of 'tradition'. But I find that St Paul wasn't. For Paul, tradition was the deposit of faith which was to be passed on to the next generation. He told the Corinthians 'For I have received from the Lord what I also delivered to you' (1 Cor 11.23). To the young Timothy he said, '. . . and what you have heard from me before many witnesses entrust to faithful men who will be able to teach others also' (2 Tim 2.2). It is frightening just how ignorant even church people can be about the essentials of the faith. The Bishop of Salisbury John Austin Baker commented recently, 'Why is it that adults in the congregation never pay so much attention as when something absolutely elementary is being explained to the children?'

2. When the church speaks publicly the last thing it seems to do is proclaim 'the mystery of God'. I found myself saying Amen to a recent comment of the Bishop of London, Dr Graham Leonard: 'What worries me about so much of what the church is saying is that it simply does not make sense . . . it isn't talking about God, it isn't talking about his love.' One aspect of it is a certain lack of confidence on the part of the church in the gospel itself. But what is even more disconcerting is the fact that the church today seems to be a bewildering array of voices saying different things. It is not a case of 'the trumpet being unclear'. More often than not it is the fact that there are a lot of differently tuned trumpets all sounding at once. And it is afflicted by timidity. Bishop Lesslie Newbigin commenting recently on the difference between the church here compared to South India, said: 'What struck me most when I came back was the timidity of the church, the unwillingness to challenge people's assumptions.'

3. Bishop Newbigin has also given valuable advice about 'engaging with the world'. Christians, he said, need to learn

to 'indwell the Bible'. Instead of viewing the Bible through the lenses of our culture and fashions, we need to 'look at the world from inside the Bible'. That is harder than it sounds. It asks a great deal from the clergy in their teaching role and on the whole they are not well trained to do it. The standard theological college course requires that ordinands jump through a series of academic hoops. When they come to the Bible they may learn the original languages, they discover a lot about its historical and cultural background, and they become aware of many of the problems the scholars have identified about dating, formation of the text and all the rest. There are hermeneutics and preaching classes. But application remains, in my view, the poor relation. Things don't improve later on unless the clergy, whose lifestyle is entirely different from most of their parishioners, don't make a conscious effort to keep their fingers on the pulse of current affairs. Karl Barth, the great German theologian, once said that Christians need to learn to pray with their Bible in one hand and the daily newspaper in the other. Some of the best trainer-vicars I know see to it that their curates read the daily papers and practise discussing the contents.

The Bishop of Warrington, Michael Henshall, says there are four kinds of clergy. There are the traditionalists, who say 'I affirm the scriptures and the creeds, and preside at Holy Communion, lead worship and guide my people as to what they should do.' There are pastor-teachers who say, 'I regard myself as a stimulator of gifts, the one who enables the laity to be effective Christians.' Some see themselves as pastors: 'I care for people, love people, and serve them in their joys and sorrows.' The fourth, he says, is a rugged customer who says to his people, 'Come on, let's go.'

The Chinese have a saying:

> Not the cry but the flight of the
> wild duck leads the flock to fly
> and to follow

The church needs clergy who are officers, not corporals. If the church founded by St Augustine isn't to go the way of the North African church of the other Augustine it will need clergy with a clear vision of what God is calling his church to be in our day, and are willing to say 'Let's go.'

*   *   *

Dear Matthew

Well, you have 'done' your first funeral. It seems inconceivable to me that someone can come out of theological college and be regarded for all intents and purposes as a fully-fledged minister with no practical training on the subject. It sounds like a teacher graduating without ever encountering a class. That no doubt is part of the reason why the early years are regarded as much training as anything else.

I notice that in helping launch a new charity to help the bereaved recently Harry Secombe commented that most clergy of the Church of England have had little or no worthwhile training in the area of bereavement counselling.

On the whole we deal with death very badly in our community. Death has become a taboo subject in just the same way as the Victorians avoided the subject of sex. We don't know what to say to people who are bereaved. If we see them coming we move over to the other side of the street. We are notoriously bad at helping children deal with death.

I will never forget a conversation I once had with a London taxi driver who turned out to be Jewish. When he found out what I did for a living he proceeded to tell me about a horrible Christian funeral he had just attended. Evidently the family were not church people, and the officiant clearly did not know them. He proceeded to tell me all about how Jews deal with death in their community. First they wish the mourners a long life. For many days after the funeral they are never left alone. Meals are brought round. A lot of thought and care goes into it.

I think that Christians could learn a lot about this from their Jewish neighbours!

*   *   *

Dear Matthew

I had to laugh when I read about your efforts to reform your parish 'house group'. From years of parish life I know the problems all too well. Parish groups are notorious for developing a life of their own. It is very difficult to get them to see themselves from a wider perspective.

I remember being in a parish where it took ages for the so-called young marrieds' group that had operated for six years to realise that they were no longer the 'young marrieds' because an entirely new generation had come on the scene. My saddest story is another former parish where no member of the Young Men's Society was under 60. There are scores of Mothers' Union branches populated largely by grand-mothers who make sure no contemporary mum comes to their meetings by running them at 3.00 p.m. when any young Mum who isn't at work is awaiting the return of the family from school.

Change in the church is one of the most painful and complex issues of our times. One interesting aspect has been the impact of charismatic renewal. Even where parishes have not been directly involved there have been ripple effects. The emphasis on the development of the gifts of the whole people of God has completely changed the relation-ship between clergy and people. Lay people expect to be involved in ministry. That has required complete re-negotiation of what clergy and laity expect of each other. It certainly requires different skills on the part of the clergy. The big question is whether or not all the activity is actually contributing to the mission of the church.

Over the last 20 years there has been a liturgical revol-ution. The Alternate Service Book 1980 (ASB) is now widely accepted. It is interesting to see how widely the Eucharist has become the centrepiece of parish worship even in traditionally evangelical or 'low' churches.

Presently the church is struggling with the issue of the ordination of women. The arguments will be bitter and with us for a while yet. Looming up too are the matters of inclusive language and relations with people from the other great world religions who now live here in the UK. Again, there is much mixed feeling about the involvement of the church in social questions.

My belief is that much of the present controversy in the life of the Church of England grows out of a very human fear of change. Show me anyone who really welcomes change. What we seem to forget is that in the Christian faith we are in the business of change:

1. We believe in a gospel that changes and transforms people. That has a dynamic influence in any parish that is serious about evangelism. Bringing in new people requires being open to new gifts being identified and channelled.
2. Being open to the Word of God requires a willingness to be open to change.

However, how are we to know if our Anglican attempts to be relevant and up-to-date represent openness to the Word of God or simply a situation where the world has squeezed us into its mould?

It is interesting to compare the way Anglicans and Roman Catholics relate to tradition. In relation to science and technology since the Enlightenment, Anglicans have had a tendency to question tradition in the face of new discoveries and developments. On the other hand the Roman Catholic Church tends to question discoveries and developments by reference to tradition.

No matter what the approach, the crucial issue is how we view revelation. Bishop Charles Gore had a brilliant, critical mind. But he displayed a humility in the face of revelation which I think is too often missing in the church today. When we don't understand God's revelation, or when we find it uncomfortable, we tend to criticise or ignore it altogether. Gore in contrast would ask: 'Where is the fault in me that means I am unable to understand?'

When we are put in a position of leadership we are often called on to be agents of change. Over the years I have found five principles which stand me in very good stead when I find myself working alongside people who are reluctant to change:

1. It is important to build up a base of support for change among key people. Your vicar is the single-most important person in this category. In a voluntary society like the church the most successful change agents seed ideas in such a way that other people think they were theirs.

2. It is best to go ahead with radical change on the basis of unanimous agreement. That is one of the beauties of the church in Africa. African Christians feel very uncomfortable with parliamentary procedures, voting and all the rest. When there is a big decision they will talk for hours until there is full agreement. That was the pattern of the early church. Believers would talk the matter out until there was complete consensus and it could be genuinely said: 'It seemed good to the Holy Spirit and to us' (Ac 15.28).

3. When people are fearful of innovation it can be helpful to suggest a trial period rather than once-for-all change. Agreeing to undertake a review will often improve the original idea. And very often once people have seen that things work, agreement to make the change permanent will come easily.

4. Review of the constitutional Aims and Objects of an organisation is often the best and most radical way to start a process of change and renewal. Many an inward-looking Mothers' Union branch has been re-vitalised through reviewing the five admirable Objects of that organisation and looking at their implications for parish and community.

5. All change agents need to be full of humility. It never does any harm for leaders to admit they were wrong. Few mistakes cannot be rectified. And there is always more than one possible solution to most problems – so be willing to listen to other people and keep a sense of perspective about your pet ideas.

*   *   *

Dear Matthew

This is to wish you all the best for your 'priesting'. I hope that the whole event will be a big encouragement to you. I'm sorry I won't be able to be there. I am sure you won't feel any different at the end – except that the hands on your head will authorise you to preside at communion. Graham at least will be relieved that he now has a colleague who can do that!

I'm not all that surprised to hear that some of your 'enlightened' former college mates are chafing about clerical clothing. I think there is a lot of muddled thinking – especially by clergy – about titles, status, and vestments. The problem grows out of a confusion between what is meant by the *priesthood* of all believers and their *ministry*. It's made worse by the fact that a lot of clergy feel anxiety about what their role is.

1. It is important to see the distinction between the priesthood of all believers and particular ministries. All believers are called to the priesthood of the whole church. We are 'a chosen race, a royal priesthood, a holy nation . . . [in order to] . . . declare the wonderful deeds of him who called you out of darkness into his marvellous light' (1 Pet 2.9). But only some are called to minister in the life of the church. The church in Antioch 'set apart' Saul and Barnabas for a special task (Ac 13.2). Ephesians 4.4ff speaks of the oneness of the body of Christ and goes on to point out that there will be separate roles (v. 7) according to the measure of Christ's gift.

2. That calling will of necessity 'separate' the Christian minister from the rest. The reference above to Saul and Barnabas suggests this. It is there even more explicitly in 2 Timothy 2.4 where the minister's role is compared to that of the soldier on service who does not get 'entangled in civilian pursuits'.

3. There is a biblical tradition that the leader at worship wore distinctive dress. This happened in the synagogue as well as the Temple. There is even a case for suggesting that

Jesus may have worn the traditional clothing of a rabbi. The point of wearing distinctive dress is not to indulge in drama and draw attention to the minister, but to make the minister more anonymous so that God alone will be glorified.

*   *   *

Dear Matthew

Your account of the pain expressed by your colleague Barbara as she witnessed your priesting has prompted me to put down some thoughts about women's ministry.

The Church of England Newspaper is reputed to be strongly in favour of the ordination of women. Yet as editor I have never once expressed my personal views on the subject except for arguing that the role of the paper is to ensure that the voices of all sides are heard and that the church should conduct the discussion in a way that honours God. It seems a bit upside down but I'd like to begin by looking at the main arguments against.

First we have what I call the iconic argument. It runs as follows: the priest presiding at the Eucharist is a symbol or expression of Christ our great High Priest. God is male. Christ was male. The priest needs to be likewise.

To me it is part of the providence of God that Christ came in male form. It is in the providence of God that he came in a particular time and culture. I have to approach that with humility and be very careful about making any suggestion that none of these things count in our day and age.

If I take the argument on its own terms I have to ask what the whole purpose of the incarnation was. God became a man, shared our life and finally died, in order that we need no longer be estranged from God but live in communion with him. If Christ had not been fully human, salvation would not have been possible.

We know that the work of Christ is just as effective for men and women. The church father Irenaus said of the incarnation: 'What Christ could not become he could not heal.' I think that says it all.

That assumes that you happen to agree that this is what being a priest is all about. And that – for me – is where the argument falls down completely.

Now we come to what has been called the 'headship' argument. The argument is that Christ has ordained that men should preside over the community of the church and that the scriptures forbid women having authority over men.

It is very easy to trade biblical texts in support of one side or the other without getting far. But I find myself on the side of those favouring women's ordination for several reasons – some biblical, some less so:

1. In the biblical account we find the subjection of women to men happened *after the fall* and as a consequence of it. However under the new creation 'there is neither Jew nor Greek, there is neither slave nor free, there is neither male nor female' (Gal 3.28) because we are all one in Christ.

2. Some of the most often quoted Pauline views on the subject are exceedingly difficult to understand and apply. In the passage (1 Tim 2.13ff) where Paul asserts male authority in the church he states that 'Adam was not deceived' (when he was) and that 'women will be saved through bearing children' (when in fact they are saved by the work of Christ).

3. The debate in the Anglican Church here in the UK is often very blinkered. The whole missionary movement of the last 150 years witnesses to the fact that God has given his blessing to the work of thousands of women in church planting and leadership.

For these reasons I believe that we should apply the Gamaliel principle: If this is of human making it will fail but '. . . if it is of God you will not be able to overthrow them (Acts 5.39). Moreover I think that the huge task of the re-evangelisation of the UK requires marshalling of the church's entire store of people and gifts.

*   *   *

Dear Matthew

I enjoyed the account of your discussion with the parishioner who was worried about the idea of the church getting involved in politics.

It's a hoary old argument and I like to imagine what would have happened to someone like Elijah if he had believed that the people of God should never be political. Can you imagine him saying 'I really mustn't confront Ahab and Jezebel over Naboth's vineyard because, after all, that is being political isn't it?'

It is right that the church should address the moral issues at stake in the life of the nation. One problem is that so many church bodies issue statements and seem to have the impression that nothing more needs to be done. It worries me, too, that often the church is unclear about why it is making statements in the first place.

The church is in the conversion business. Bishop Stephen Neill once said that conversion has three elements: conversion to Christ, conversion to the church, and conversion to the world.

Conversion to Christ is fundamental. It means accepting and celebrating the fact that by his life, death and resurrection Christ has brought us into communion with God. In that relationship we trust in him and seek to follow his ways in every detail of our lives.

Conversion to the church is often neglected in our thinking. Christianity is not a private or individualistic matter. It is expressed in community in which people are members one of another, support each other, and help the weak. It is a sign to the world of God's love.

Conversion to the world does not mean being worldly. It grows out of the fact that God sent his Son into the world to save it. It is all too easy for Christians to live to themselves and be pre-occupied with their own inner-life. The opposite danger is becoming so pre-occupied with social involvement that we lose our specifically Christian cutting edge. Being converted to the world is having our perspective changed so that we look outward and are not totally pre-occupied with our own personal concerns.

There is a lot we can learn from the early church when it comes to witness in our increasingly post-Christian society. We need to be both proclaiming the faith and meeting human need – as Charles Colson put it, being the 'little platoons of society'. During the early decades of the church there were many apologists who thought up powerful arguments for the Christian faith against the pagan thinkers of the day. That certainly had an impact in its own way. But what came over with even greater power as far as ordinary people were concerned was the way Christians cared. In second century Rome the lot of abandoned widows could be terrible. The tiny Christian community did something about it and the news of it spread far and wide. When plague hit the city of Carthage pagan households would throw infected people into the streets to die. Christians – even the bishop – were to be seen on the streets, caring for them, taking them into their homes. This sort of action gave the church such credibility that when the Emperor Julian tried to bring back paganism he said that the success of this enterprise depended on the old religion learning to care like the Christians.

Christianity has a moral power that can change people and communities. At Hyde Park Corner one Sunday a heckler interrupted a Christian preacher. Pointing to a tramp he said, 'Socialism could put a new suit on that man.'

'Yes,' said the preacher. 'But Christ could put a new man into that suit.'

**Two more international bestsellers
from Highland Books**

ORDERING
YOUR
PRIVATE WORLD

with Study Guide

by

GORDON MacDONALD

Awarded the Gold Medallion for the Best Devotional Book of the Year.

'*One of the most helpful books I've read in twenty years.*'
Gavin Reid

'*I wish that I had read it years ago.*'

Billy Graham

A new edition to help you obtain the maximum benefit from a life-changing message.

HIGHLAND BOOKS

RESTORING YOUR SPIRITUAL PASSION

by

GORDON MacDONALD

We are working harder, playing longer, buying more and yet we are enjoying life less. Why is there so much dissatisfaction with our lives? *Restoring Your Spiritual Passion* gives the reasons and answers to our dilemma.

Here are practical steps to help you escape the pervasive sense of spiritual tiredness that has settled into your life. They will re-open the 'rivers of living water' and help quench your inner thirst.

'All who mean business with God could find their batteries recharged by getting to grips with this book.'
Christian Arena

HIGHLAND BOOKS